Explorations in Language Study
General Editors:
Peter Doughty   Geoffrey Thornton

ACCENT, DIALECT AND THE SCHOOL

Peter Trudgill

EDWARD ARNOLD

© Peter Trudgill 1975

First published 1975
by Edward Arnold (publishers) Ltd
25 Hill Street, London W1X 8LL

ISBN 0 7131 1983 7

Explorations in Language Study

Language in the Junior School
E. Ashworth

Language and Community
E. A. and P. S. Doughty

Language Study, the Teacher and the Learner
P. S. Doughty and G. M. Thornton

Language, Brain and Interactive Processes
R. S. Gurney

Explorations in the Functions of Language
M. A. K. Halliday

Learning How to Mean: Explorations in the Development of Language
M. A. K. Halliday

English as a Second and Foreign Language
B. Harrison

Language in Bilingual Communities
D. Sharp

Language, Experience and School
G. M. Thornton

Printed in Great Britain by Butler & Tanner Ltd
Frome and London

General Introduction

In the course of our efforts to develop a linguistic focus for work in English language, which was published as *Language in Use*, we came to realize the extent of the growing interest in what we would call a linguistic approach to language. Lecturers in Colleges and Departments of Education see the relevance of such an approach in the education of teachers. Many teachers in schools and in Colleges of Further Education recognise that 'educational failure is primarily *linguistic* failure', and are turning to Linguistic Science for some kind of exploration and practical guidance. Many of those now exploring the problems of relationships, community or society, from a sociological or psychological point of view wish to make use of a linguistic approach to the language in so far as it is relevant to these problems.

We were conscious of the wide divergence between the aims of the linguist, primarily interested in describing language as a system for organizing 'meanings', and the needs of those who now wanted to gain access to the insights that resulted from that interest. In particular, we were aware of the wide gap that separated the literature of academic Linguistics from the majority of those who wished to find out what Linguistic Science might have to say about language and the use of language.

Out of this experience emerged our own view of that much-used term, 'Language Study', developed initially in the chapters of *Exploring Language*, and now given expression in this series. Language Study is not a subject, but a process, which is why the series is called *Explorations in Language Study*. Each exploration is focused upon a meeting point between the insights of Linguistic Science, often in conjunction with other social sciences, and the linguistic questions raised by the study of a particular aspect of individual behaviour or human society.

I

The volumes in the series have a particular relevance to the role of language in teaching and learning. The editors intend that they should make a basic contribution to the literature of Language Study, doing justice equally to the findings of the academic disciplines involved and the practical needs of those who now want to take a linguistic view of their own particular problems of language and the use of language.

Peter Doughty
Geoffrey Thornton

Contents

3

Introduction

A major objective of *Explorations in Language Study* is to put into the hands of those who are responsible for the fate of pupils in school a number of studies which will show how pupils learn and use language to live. We are convinced that teachers can only make sense of their work in school if they are aware of pupils, first and foremost, as human beings who have learnt to use language in the process of learning how to live—as members of a family, a community and a society. In the two collections of Professor Halliday's papers, *Explorations in the Functions of Language* and *Explorations in the Development of Language,* we offer the teacher what seems to us the most convincing account of language as a complex product of individual, social and cultural experience at present available to us. In Eric Ashworth's *Language in the Junior School,* or Anne and Peter Doughty's *Using Language in Use,* we offer a practical discussion of the 'how to' of teaching the mother tongue, a discussion which draws its strength from its roots in this same way of looking at language.

Between this theoretical account of language as a social and cultural artifact and the practical discussion of how we should approach our work with language in the classroom, however, lies the crucial area of attitude, the teacher's attitudes towards, and assumptions about, language and its use. It seems to me enormously important for the future teaching of the mother tongue, and its use as the primary medium for teaching and learning across the whole range of the curriculum, that the Bullock Report has taken as its title, not 'Reading', or 'English in Education', but 'Language for Life'. What this implies for

---

* *Using Language in Use: a teachers' guide to language work in the classroom.* Edward Arnold, 1974.

the teacher's attitude towards the part language plays in the life of his pupils the Report makes absolutely explicit:

> ... The aim is not to alienate the child from a form of language with which he has grown up and which serves him efficiently in the speech community of his neighbourhood ... we emphasise that the teacher should start where the child is and should accept the language he brings to school ... and this takes us firmly to the need for an explicit knowledge by the teacher of how language operates.

In *Language and Community*, my wife and I present a general account of the way in which 'a form of language with which [the child] has grown up' can so adequately supply his linguistic needs '... in the speech community of his neighbourhood'. Now, Peter Trudgill adds to the series an immensely valuable account of one particular, and quite crucial, aspect of every speech community, its accent and dialect, an account which considers what we should understand by these two much abused terms and how our understanding of them can directly affect the language climate of the school.

I say 'immensely valuable', because the question of accent and dialect appears to cause more trouble and distress, both to teachers and their pupils, than almost any other. I cannot think of a single group of teachers or student teachers with whom I have worked that has not produced at least one question about accent and dialect, or revealed attitudes towards them that would be harmful to their pupils. As Peter Trudgill shows, what these attitudes unfortunately so often reveal is an approach to the pupil's own ways of speaking that would almost certainly '... alienate the child from a form of language with which he has grown up'.

It has to be accepted, however, that our attitudes to language are deep-rooted and that we are often highly resistant to alternative ways of looking at language. Peter Trudgill attempts to meet this situation by presenting, as clearly and untechnically as possible, a very well documented account of the nature and function of accent and dialect, what we can say about each one of them from a linguistic point of view, and how this relates to our customary habit of using accent and dialect as indexes of personal character or academic potential. In effect, he offers us a 'plain man's guide to the true character of accent and dialect'. In the process, he suggests that we must learn to reconsider judgements

6

of accent and dialect which conceal, often unintentionally, a judgement of class, or status, or intelligence, within what appears to be an innocuously 'objective' assessment of 'a form of language'.

On this question of the teacher's judgement of ways of speaking, the Bullock Report is quite explicit:

> . . . We believe that a child's accent should be accepted and that to attempt to suppress it is irrational and neither humane nor necessary. . . .

What *Accent, Dialect and the School* can do for the reader who may be sceptical of the validity of this statement, and wonders what grounds there are for so positive an assertion, is to show him just why the 'attempt to suppress [a child's accent] is irrational and neither humane nor necessary'. In this way, it seems to me to exemplify, in this quite crucial area of our attitude to language, an area so vital to the creation of a supportive language climate in schools, just that 'explicit knowledge . . . of how language operates' the teacher now needs.

Peter Doughty

Preface

This book is an attempt to bring a number of linguistic concepts and results from linguistic research to bear on certain educational problems connected with language. It is especially concerned with problems arising out of non-standard dialects and low-status accents, with particular reference to reading and writing, but it also includes discussion of other matters involving language, such as 'verbal deprivation' and the development of verbal skills. I have attempted to discuss all these topics as simply and non-technically as possible.

Pioneering work on the subject of non-standard dialects in education has been carried out by scholars active in the field of sociolinguistics in the U.S.A., and it is clear to me that without the work of American linguists, notably William Labov, Roger Shuy, Ralph Fasold and Walt Wolfram, this book could not have appeared in its present form, since I have drawn heavily on their research and ideas. This text, however, is aimed specifically at British audiences, and I have tried wherever possible to include illustrations from different varieties of British English taken from my own work and that of others in this country.

Many of the ideas presented here I have developed as a result of talking to and with groups of teachers, in different parts of the country, on topics such as 'language and social class' and 'socio-linguistics and education'—and I have found that the interchange of ideas which always takes place on these occasions has been very useful indeed. But, in writing this book, I was still very conscious of the fact that, as a linguist with no classroom experience, my views on the educational applications of linguistic research might not in all cases have been entirely sound. I am therefore very grateful indeed to all the teachers who have helped me in the preparation of this text and supplied me with very valuable advice derived from their own experience: they have all done their best to keep my thinking on the right lines. I would particularly like to acknowledge the invaluable assistance I have received from Chris Lawrence, who has made a number of important contributions at different points, and the considerable number of recommendations and suggestions for improvement I have received from Richard Dawson, Robin McClelland and Sandra Trudgill. Without them I would not have ventured to publish what follows.

I am also very grateful to my colleagues in the Department of Linguistic Science at the University of Reading, Paul Fletcher and Michael Garman, for reading and checking the manuscript for inaccuracies and for suggesting a number of improvements, as well as others who have helped in the same way, especially Arne Kjell Foldvik.

Peter Trudgill

1 Diversity in Language

Many countries in the world, particularly in parts of Africa and Asia, have several tens or even hundreds of languages spoken within their frontiers. In comparison, the linguistic situation in Britain is obviously much less complex. Everybody, or nearly everybody, speaks English. In fact, from a linguistic point of view, Britain might appear at first sight to be a very uninteresting place. It is true, of course, that the language situation is not entirely straightforward: there are speakers of Gaelic in the Highlands and Islands of Scotland, and many Welsh speakers in Wales. But the vast majority of these people can and do speak English as well. It is also true that there are numbers of immigrants in this country from parts of the Commonwealth and elsewhere who do not have English as their mother tongue, but most of them, or at least their children, seem to be learning English rapidly. There is certainly no real need for anyone visiting or living in this country to know any language other than English. For many purposes, Britain is monolingual.

However, this does not in fact mean that this country is a linguistically homogeneous or uniform place. While most people do speak English, it is far from being the case that they all speak it alike. As many of us are well aware, there is actually a great deal of variation in the way in which different people speak and use English. This variation has for a long time been a source of interest and, sometimes, amusement. Many of us, for example, are rather fascinated by the different types of English that are spoken in different parts of the country, and some of us make jokes about it. But linguistic diversity is also a cause for concern for many of those who are working in education. Does it matter if a teacher in a southern school has a north-country accent? Does a Cockney teacher set his children a bad example? If a child uses grammatical constructions not found in grammar books is this wrong or merely different? If a pupil writes

He did not want none

should we correct it or leave it alone? If we allow a child to say *ammer* instead of *hammer*, will he suffer in later life?

It is the purpose of this book to attempt to answer questions like these, and to deal in general with educational problems arising out of language and linguistic diversity. Much of the book is based on research that has been carried out by people working in the field of linguistics—the scientific study of language—as well as in education and psychology. In this chapter we shall discuss, briefly, the nature and causes of linguistic variation in English, and then go on to discuss some of the terms used by linguists to describe it. In the following chapters we shall discuss the problems themselves and some of their possible solutions.

1. Variation in English

Much of the linguistic variation to be found in this country has a regional basis. People from Aberdeen do not sound like Devonians when they speak, and the English of Liverpudlians is easily distinguishable from that of Londoners. Often this is simply a matter of pronunciation, but it can also be a matter of grammar and vocabulary. If you hear someone say:

What like was it?

it is reasonable to suppose that they come from somewhere in Scotland, since people in England and Wales normally say:

What was it like?

People in the north of England and most of the Midlands will generally say:

Do you want your clothes washing?

while the normal form for speakers from Scotland and the south of England would be:

Do you want your clothes washed?

Many other examples of this type of regional variation could be given, and anyone who has travelled very much will be able to supply his own.

There is also, however, some variation which is not regional. Even in a single locality such as London or Liverpool we find that people from different social backgrounds speak different kinds of English. Doctors do not sound like dockers anywhere, and building workers do not speak like business-men. There are no hard and fast rules about this, but if you hear someone say:

I ain't got it yet   or   *I've no got it yet*

he is more likely to be a docker than a doctor. Doctors, in most people's experience, are more likely to say:

I haven't got it yet
or   *I've not got it yet*
or   *I don't have it yet.*

There will also be differences in pronunciation and, to a certain extent, vocabulary, and most of us are sufficiently aware of differences of this sort to be able to place somebody socially by their speech in a reasonably accurate kind of way.

The position is further complicated by the fact that, even within the English of individual speakers, considerable variation occurs, regardless of their social background. This variation is often due to the different social contexts in which a person may have to speak, and the different types of language he produces will normally be quite closely related to the relative formality or informality of a particular situation. To say:

I have insufficient financial resources for the journey

would sound appropriate in a formal situation. But for most people it would be out of place, except as a joke, if it were said at home or to close friends. In these circumstances

I haven't got enough money for the trip

or something similar would be much more usual. Pronunciation can also change, for many speakers, from situation to situation— a 'telephone voice' is a good example.

Britain, then, is by no means linguistically uniform. The English spoken here is subject to considerable regional, social and stylistic (formal–informal) variation—and English is not at all unusual in this respect. Linguistic heterogeneity in monolingual communities appears to be universal. It seems to be the counterpart in language of social diversity, and since all societies, even the smallest, are internally differentiated in various ways, all languages are variable. We can find regional variation in Icelandic, for example, even though this is spoken by only about 200,000 people, and in Faroese, with no more than 35,000 speakers.

2. The causes of variation in English

How does this linguistic diversity arise? Why doesn't everybody in Britain speak English in the same way? There are no straight-forward answers to these questions, but one of the most important factors is that language is a dynamic kind of phenomenon. Languages are always changing, and English is just as much subject to linguistic change as any other language. We are not really sure why this is, but no language ever remains entirely static. It is fairly obvious that Shakespeare's English is very different from the modern language; the language of Chaucer is so different as to be quite difficult to understand; and King Alfred's English does actually require translation. Linguistic change appears to be inevitable. It can be slowed down, particularly by universal literacy. (The written language, involved as it is with the making of relatively permanent records, is generally more conservative than speech.) But it cannot be stopped. Letter-writers to *The Times* and others opposed to innovations and changes in language today are fighting a losing battle, just as their counterparts were in previous centuries. Many features of the modern language that we now take for granted and find perfectly acceptable, such as the grammatical construction in:

> *The house is being built next year*

were bitterly opposed by certain critics when they first made an appearance in English. And there is no reason to suppose that the same kind of cycle of *innovation–resistance–acceptance* will not continue to operate in future. Linguistic change is a natural phenomenon and does not imply 'decay' or 'corruption' as was often maintained in the past.

Words often change their meaning, and it is very unrealistic to claim, as some people do, that a particular word 'really' means something else—usually an older meaning. We all use very many words which formerly meant something else. A good example of this is the word *aggravate*. Some people feel that this word 'really' means 'to make more serious' (because of its Latin etymology) and that the more recent meaning of 'to irritate' is therefore 'wrong'. It is simply the case, however, that *aggravate*, while

14

preserving its original meaning, has also acquired another. Most people use it to mean 'to irritate', so that is what it does mean. The English language has lost nothing. Misunderstanding will not occur, since 'to aggravate a situation' (with an abstract object) and 'to aggravate a person' (with an animate object) can never be confused. And even if the original meaning were lost, English still has a number of other words that could replace *aggravate* in different contexts. In some cases, too, change can even mean 'growth'—when language is adapted, consciously or subconsciously, to handle new topics and ideas.

As a language changes, it may well change in different ways in different places. No one who speaks a particular language can remain in close contact with *all* the other speakers of that language. Social and geographical barriers to communication as well as sheer distance mean that a change that starts amongst speakers in one particular locality will probably spread only to other areas with which these speakers are in close contact. This is what has happened over the centuries in the case of the languages we now call English and German. Two thousand years ago the Germanic peoples living in what is now, for the most part, Germany could understand one another perfectly well. However, when many of them migrated to England they did not remain in close contact with those who stayed behind. The result, to simplify somewhat, was that different linguistic changes took place in the two areas independently so that today English and German, while clearly related languages, are not mutually intelligible. There was presumably a certain amount of inevitability about this process, since speakers usually need to remain intelligible only to those people they normally communicate with, and, until quite recently, close and frequent communication between England and Germany was not possible. But this also means that the same kind of process is unlikely to be repeated in such an extreme form in the case of different variants of modern English. American and British English have been geographically separated, and diverging linguistically, for 300 years or so, but the divergence is not very great because of the density of the communication between the two speech communities, particularly since the advent of modern transport and communications facilities. In other words, linguistic change in English will continue, but it is very unlikely indeed (barring prolonged world-wide catastrophes) that this will lead to a decrease in the mutual intelligibility of different varieties of English. That is, it is not legitimate to argue that change in English is a bad thing because it will lead to a breakdown in communication. It will not—so long as all English speakers need and are able to keep in touch with each other.

In fact, if anything, the reverse is more likely, since change does not necessarily take place in a 'divergent' direction. Where two groups of speakers develop closer social contacts than they had previously, their language is quite likely to converge. This appears to have happened in Jamaica, where the language spoken today is much more like British English than it was 200 years ago.

And even where change is of the divergent type, it should not necessarily be assumed that this is a bad thing. From many points of view, of course, it is true that a large increase in linguistic diversity on a world-wide scale would be unfortunate. Particularly in the sphere of international politics, it is desirable that different peoples should be able to communicate as freely and accurately as possible. But at the same time it is also valid to argue that the maintenance of a certain number of linguistic barriers to communication is a good thing. These barriers, although penetrable, ensure the survival of different language communities. And the separation of the world's population into different groups speaking different languages helps the growth of cultural diversity, which in turn can lead to opportunities for the development of alternative modes of exploring possibilities for social, political and technological progress. A world where everyone spoke the same language could be a very dull and stagnant place.

Within Britain, then, different regional and social variants of English have developed because—or at least partly because—different linguistic changes have taken place in different parts of the country and in different sections of the community. Londoners have not generally had close contacts with Glaswegians, and for that reason the two speak very different types of English. Dockers, typically, have more social contacts with other dockers than with doctors—which also leads to the growth of linguistic differences.

Geographical barriers can also play an important role. Until quite recently, for example, the Fens were swampy and difficult to cross, which made them a substantial barrier to social contacts and therefore to the spread of linguistic changes. One result of this is that a number of linguistic boundaries run from the Wash through the Fens, between Lincolnshire and Norfolk. In Norfolk, for instance, people have a 'long *a*' in words like *glass* and *path*, and pronounce *cud* and *could* with different vowels. In Lincoln-

16

shire *glass* and *path* have a 'short *a*' and *cud* and *could* are pronounced the same.

Once linguistic differences have arisen in this way they are
often maintained or even exaggerated because of the symbolic
value they can have in signalling an individual's or a group's
identity. For example, given that it is well known that northerners
and southerners pronounce words like *glass* and *path* in different
ways, there are many northerners who will not want to change
over to using a 'long *a*' in words of this type. This could be, as it
were, letting the side down: it is part of one's identity as a
'northerner' to have a 'short *a*' in *glass* and *path*, and to change
the pronunciation would be to attempt to change the identity.
Factors of this type can be very important in an educational
situation, and resistance by children to the adoption of new forms
of language can often be for such reasons—of regional and, in
particular, social and personal identity. (We shall discuss this
point at greater length in Chapter 4.)

3. Dialect and standard English

Before we can begin to discuss the educational implications of
linguistic diversity it is necessary to discuss briefly the labels we
shall be applying to different kinds of language in the rest of this
book. This is important because terms like *dialect* and *accent* can
be rather emotive and even embarrassing unless their use is
clearly defined. In the chapters that follow we shall use the
term *variety* to refer to any 'kind of language' that we happen to
want to discuss, in a neutral kind of way, without prejudging
any issues. The term *dialect*, on the other hand, means any variety
which is grammatically different from any other, as well, perhaps,
as having a different vocabulary or pronunciation.

'Grammatically different' here refers to the fact that different
dialects may have, for example, different forms for the past tense
of certain verbs, such as *I wrote it* as opposed to *I writ it*; or different types of sentence construction, such as *I want to go* as opposed
to *I want for to go*—and so on. We shall discuss grammatical
differences further below, p. 44.

This definition of *dialect* has two important implications. First,
all of us who speak English are dialect speakers; we all speak at
least one dialect of English. The term *dialect*, in other words, is not
reserved for application only to old-fashioned or rustic forms of
speech. Secondly, differences in pronunciation alone are not

17

sufficient to make for differences in dialect. Pronunciation differences make merely for a difference of *accent* (see below).

One of the most important varieties of English is that dialect which is widely known as *standard English*. Standard English is the dialect used by most speakers who would consider themselves to be 'educated'; it is normally used in writing and on radio and television; it is the form of English normally taught to foreign learners; and, in many important respects, it is the language of British schools—a fact that we shall be discussing at some length in Chapter 4.

It is not actually possible to *define* standard English, any more than it is possible to define any other dialect. All we can do is to give a few examples of usages that are clearly either standard English or not standard English.

STANDARD ENGLISH	VARIOUS NON-STANDARD DIALECTS
I did it	I done it
He hasn't gone	He hasn't went
I like him	I likes him
He wants them	He want them
You saw her	You seen her
Those people	Them people

Some people may be somewhat surprised to see standard English described as a dialect, but since it is grammatically different from other dialects, as the above examples show, and since dialects are defined in terms of grammatical difference, it is quite legitimate to do so.

We now have to recognise two further things. First, standard English has nothing to do with pronunciation. (This of course follows from the definition of dialect given above.) Secondly, standard English, like all other dialects, is subject to internal variation. It has, first of all, regional variants. American standard English is not identical with English standard English, and Scottish standard English may be different again.

AMERICAN STANDARD ENG.	He'd gotten it
ENGLISH STANDARD ENG.	He'd got it
SCOTTISH STANDARD ENG.	You had a good time, hadn't you?
ENGLISH STANDARD ENG.	You had a good time, didn't you?

It is important to note here that we can use the term *dialect* in a pragmatic or *ad hoc* way to be as specific as necessary for particu-

18

lar purposes: we can talk about *standard English* as a dialect, but we can also talk about *standard British English* and *standard English English* as dialects, with equal validity. In the same kind of way we can discuss the dialects *Yorkshire English, West Riding English, Bradford English* and *middle-class Bradford English,* if we so desire. The point is that dialects are not homogeneous, fixed entities with well-defined labels. Neither do they have clear-cut well-established boundaries; marginal features often occur which cannot be assigned with any confidence to one dialect rather than another.

4. Style

The second source of internal variation within standard English is that it is, again like all other dialects, subject to stylistic differentiation. We have already noted that different degrees of formality in particular situations will produce different varieties of language. Varieties of this type are known as *styles,* and all dialects contain different stylistic variants. Styles are normally signalled by the use of certain words rather than others. In the example we gave above, for instance, *trip* and *not enough* (see p. 13) indicate a style more informal than *journey* and *insufficient.* Dialects, on the other hand, are defined in terms of grammar—which means that speakers can employ very colloquial styles, including slang vocabulary and swear-words, and still be using standard English. For example:

> *I'm bloody knackered*

may be part of a conversation in standard English (in an informal style, of course), while

> *I be very tired*

cannot be considered as an example of the standard English dialect.

WRITTEN AND SPOKEN LANGUAGE

Other things being equal, the language of writing tends to be couched in more formal styles than spoken language—although this is more of a tendency than a rule. But there are also other differences between written and spoken language which may be more important for those concerned with English in the school.

It is easier, for instance, to use more complex syntactic patterns in writing than in speech because writing allows for checking and rephrasing and does not impose so much of a burden on the memory. In many ways writing also tends to have more prestige than the spoken language, probably because it provides a permanent record and is associated with literature, law, education and so on. Linguists, on the other hand, normally dissociate themselves from views of this sort. They point out that writing is parasitic upon speech in that it is simply a way of recording the spoken language in an enduring, visual form. Both in the history of particular languages, and in the development of the individual human being, speech comes first, writing second, and there are very many languages in the world that are spoken but not written. From the point of view of the study of language, then, the spoken language is primary, and the written language is a special, secondary development. For this reason (and we shall discuss this point later), appeals to the written language in disputes about, say, the pronunciation of certain words are generally unfounded and misconceived.

5. Accent

Differences in pronunciation, as we have already seen, make for differences of *accent*. This means that, as in the case of dialect, absolutely everybody speaks with an accent—an accent is not something odd or peculiar but something that we all have.

Some people confuse accent with 'voice'. Strictly speaking, voice refers to those aspects of a person's speech which are due to the physiological make-up of his vocal tract and which are peculiar to him. Many people have the same accent, but no two people have the same voice—it is a speaker's voice which we recognise when we hear him talking without seeing him.

The distinction we have made between dialect and accent means that it is in theory possible to speak any dialect with any accent. In practice, this is something that happens frequently with standard English. The vast majority of people who speak standard English do so with various types of regional accent. On the other hand, there are some standard English speakers who have an accent which, although it is clearly British, is, within Britain, not regional. This is the accent which linguists call R.P. ('received pronunciation'), and which is also known as 'B.B.C. English', 'the Queen's English' and 'public-school accent'. It is the accent employed by B.B.C. national news-readers, and is typically used by pupils and ex-pupils of the large Public Schools. It, too, is internally differentiated, so that, for instance, older members of the aristocracy and younger television announcers do not sound exactly the same. But its most salient characteristic is that its speakers do not betray, even to a slight extent, their geographical origins in their pronunciation. On the other hand, they certainly do betray their social status—as does everybody else. This is because of the relationship that exists in Britain between dialect and accent, on the one hand, and social and regional background, on the other (see fig. 1). At the 'bottom' of

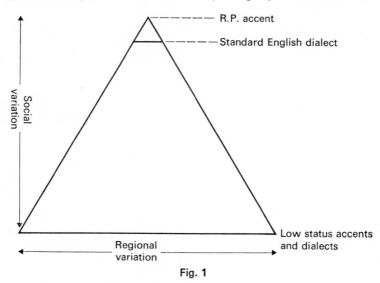

Fig. 1

the social scale we can find a wide range of geographical dialects and accents which can be heard to change gradually from place to place as one moves across the country from the south of England to the north of Scotland. At the other end of the scale we find standard English, with its small regional variations, together with either R.P. (which has variation but no *regional* variation) or moderately regional accents, depending on how near the 'top' the speaker is. At intermediate social levels we find accents and dialects which are more or less regional depending on the level. School-teachers from Newcastle and Bristol will not speak English alike, but they will sound more similar than, say, most factory workers from the same two places.

6. Drawing boundaries

In the case of both regional and social variation it has to be pointed out that it is hardly ever possible to draw a clear dividing line between one dialect or accent and another. Dialects and accents are not discrete or separate entities. We can say, if we like, that Yorkshire dialect becomes Lancashire dialect at the county boundary, but from a linguistic point of view this is purely arbitrary. Similarly we cannot, linguistically, say that a middle-class accent starts here and a working-class accent stops there. In all cases what we are really faced with is a regional or social continuum. This is something of a problem because most of us *perceive* linguistic varieties as if they were discrete. We make statements like 'John and Bill come from Liverpool, but John's got a Liverpool accent and Bill hasn't' when the true state of affairs, measured objectively from a linguistic point of view, is probably simply that Bill tends to have fewer recognisably Liverpudlian features in his pronunciation than John. Similarly, we tend to employ descriptive labels for varieties as if we were sure about exactly what they referred to, with no possibility of doubtful or intermediate cases. We use terms like 'Birmingham accent', 'Cockney', and 'Lancashire dialect' as if we could draw rings round varieties and treat them in an unambiguous either-or kind of way, when in fact linguistic varieties are almost always a question of relative more-or-less. In this book we shall continue to use labels like this, as if they were descriptions of separate, homogeneous units, because it is often convenient to do so, but it must always be borne in mind that this is a simplification and distortion of the more complex facts.

LANGUAGE

This same problem applies again to the term *language*. We are used to employing the phrase *the English language* as if it referred to a well-defined, self-contained unit. In actual fact the position is more complex than this. Those familiar with Romance languages (languages derived historically from Latin) may know that at the level of regional dialects there is no clear break between, say, French and Italian—any more than there is between Lancashire and Yorkshire English. French and Italian just merge into one another. There is a continuum of dialects that stretches from the north of France to the south of Italy which pays no attention to national frontiers. The same is true of the Germanic languages,

Dutch and German. We refer to certain varieties as 'Dutch dialects' and others as 'German dialects' only because they are spoken in Holland and Germany respectively. Dialects spoken in the west of Holland and those spoken in the south-east of Germany are not mutually intelligible, but because of the intervening continuum of regional dialects they are connected with each other by a chain of mutual intelligibility. The dividing line between 'Dutch' and 'German' at the national frontier is, once again, linguistically arbitrary.

Similar problems also occur with English, especially when we come to consider those language varieties spoken in the West Indies. Are these varieties 'English' or not? From a purely linguistic point of view we cannot answer this question in any sensible kind of way. Here again we are presented with a linguistic continuum, although a social (rather than geographical) one in this case, ranging from something that is clearly English at one end of the West Indian social scale, to something that is not readily intelligible to British English speakers at the other. We will, however, discuss this problem more fully in a later chapter.

In any case, we have to recognise that, when we talk about the English language, we are discussing something that is rather blurred at the edges, and internally very diverse. There is really, that is, no such thing as *the* English language.

2 Good and bad language

It is very difficult to say exactly how many languages there are in the world. Apart from the purely practical problems of obtaining reliable information from all over the earth, there is also the fact that, because of the 'boundaries and continua' problem that we have already discussed, it is very often not possible to decide what is a separate language and what is not. There are certainly, in any case, a few thousand.

During the past several decades, people working in linguistics have studied a good proportion of the world's languages—although not as many of them nor in such great detail as they would like. From this study it has emerged that there are no linguistic reasons for saying that any language is superior to any other. All languages, that is, are equally 'good'. There is no way of evaluating any language more favourably than any other. Linguists have found that all languages are complex systems which are equally valid as means of communication. Each language meets the communication needs of its speakers in an entirely adequate way, and, if these needs change, then the language changes with them. In other words, there is no such thing as a 'primitive' language. Languages spoken in communities technologically not so advanced as our own are linguistically no different from those spoken in the more fully industrialised nations. All the world's languages appear to have evolved to an equivalent stage of development. Languages spoken by isolated hill-tribes in Papua, say, are in every way as ordered and complex as English, French and the other European languages. (English speakers trying to learn such a language might be tempted to say that it was *more* complex—but this would simply be due to learning difficulties caused by large differences between the two languages.)

24

The view that no one language is better than any other runs counter to the thinking of many people. Value judgements are frequently passed on the relative merits of languages such as French, English and German. People will claim, for instance, that there are things you can say in French which 'English is just incapable of expressing'. Adjectives like 'rich', 'subtle', 'expressive' and 'flexible' are employed in attempts to prove the superiority of one or the other. Sometimes the motives for this kind of activity appear to be nationalistic. A letter-writer to a large British newspaper recently claimed that 'in the English language we have the best medium of communication in the world'. Other examples seem to be due to more praiseworthy causes such as, say, an English scholar's love for the French language. In all cases, views of this type have no basis in fact.

It appears to linguists that all languages are not only equally complex and structured. They are also no different in their expressive capabilities. There is nothing that you can say in one language that you cannot express in another. (If there was, translation and interpreting would become impossible.) It is true that languages differ. But they differ only in what they *have to* say, not in what they *can* say. If you are speaking German, for example, you have to specify whether a friend is male (*Freund*) or female (*Freundin*). In English you are not obliged to do this (*friend* includes both sexes), but you can if you wish (*woman-friend; male friend*, and so on).

It is also true that languages differ in terms of what they can say *in single words*. There may be words in French, for example, which have nuances their English counterparts do not have. But these nuances can be expressed in English, by circumlocutions, intonation patterns, and in other ways. Similarly, there is no word in English for 'to make possible'. In German there is: *ermöglichen*. But this does not mean that the English language is in any way deficient or inferior to German. The idea can be expressed perfectly adequately in English by the phrase 'make possible' or in other ways. This does require more words than the German. But there are also some things which can be said in one word in English which require two or more in German. Differences like this between two languages balance each other out.

We also have to concede, of course, that some languages have more fully developed vocabularies on some topics than other languages do. But this is simply a reflection of the needs of the speakers of those languages. English is not inadequate because it has fewer words for snow than Eskimo, or fewer words for reindeer than Lappish. And if Amerindian languages spoken in the Brazilian jungle have no words for *television* or *relativity*, this simply means they do not have TV, and that they do not know what relativity is.

The fact that no one language is 'better' than any other is important for the role of language in education. This is because the same thing is equally true of different varieties of the same language. Just as there is no linguistic reason for arguing that Gaelic is superior to Chinese, so no English dialect can be claimed to be linguistically superior or inferior to any other. All English dialects are equally complex, structured and valid linguistic systems. There is no linguistic evidence whatsoever for suggesting that one dialect is more 'expressive' or 'logical' than any other, or for postulating that there are any 'primitive', 'inadequate' or 'debased' English dialects.

Differences between English dialects, as we have already seen, are principally rather small grammatical differences. This means that 'translation' between one dialect and another causes no problems at all. It is simply a question of converting one grammatical form into its equivalent in the other dialect. Now languages like English and Chinese have very different grammars and vocabularies indeed, but we recognise that, although translation is a complex affair, anything that can be said in English can also be said in Chinese. It should therefore be clear that the relatively very much smaller grammatical differences between English dialects will cause no differences in expressive capabilities whatsoever. There is nothing you can do or say in one dialect that you cannot say in any other dialect.

It is true that different dialects do have different words. In many cases it is simply a matter of regional equivalents (English *cupboard*, Scottish *press*). In other cases it happens that some dialects have words which are not found in others. This again just reflects the needs of particular speakers. Moorland Yorkshire dialects, for example, might have hill sheep-farming terms which Hertfordshire dialects do not have. But if it ever became necessary for Hertfordshire speakers to talk about these things, they would acquire the necessary words, either by borrowing them from elsewhere, or by developing them themselves. New vocabulary is easily acquired, and there is no necessary connection between particular vocabulary items and sets of grammatical forms.

26

One implication of this is that any subject can be dealt with in any dialect. There is no reason why nuclear physics should not be discussed in Cumberland dialect, international economics in Cornish dialect, or greyhound racing in standard English. As an example, we can cite a passage from an anthropology text-book, 'translated' into a non-standard West of England dialect:

> Social anthropology be a title used in England to designate a department of the larger subject of anthropology. On the continent a different terminology prevails. There when people speaks of anthropology, what to us is the entire study of man, they has in mind only what us calls physical anthropology, the biological study of man. What us calls social anthropology would be referred to on the continent as either ethnology or sociology. Being a branch of the wider subject of anthropology, social anthropology be generally taught in connection with its other branches: physical anthropology, ethnology, prehistoric archaeology, and sometimes general linguistics and human geography. As the last two subjects seldom figures in degree and diploma courses in anthropology in this country I don't say no more about them.

Many people, of course, will find this strange and probably amusing, as it is very *unusual* to discuss (and particularly write about) anthropology in any dialect other than standard English. The point is, however, that it is perfectly *possible*.

Many people in this country will find it hard to accept that all English dialects are equally 'good'. They may be prepared to concede that a Lancashire dialect is no better than a Yorkshire dialect, and vice versa. But they will be reluctant to believe that standard English is simply no better and no worse than any other dialect. In fact there is a very widely held—although erroneous— view that standard English is *the* English language. This inevitably leads to the belief that all other dialects are deviations from the norm, and, often, that these deviations represent 'corruptions' due to ignorance, carelessness, laziness or stupidity. Since standard English is *the* English language, these people believe that to speak it and write it is *good*, and to use any other dialect is *bad*. From a linguistic point of view these arguments do not hold. First, we have already seen that there is no way in which one variety of language can be considered superior to another. Secondly, it is entirely inaccurate to regard standard English as representing an 'uncorrupted norm' and all other dialects as deviants. Historically speaking, standard English developed out of the dialects spoken in the south-east of England, and as the language of the court and government it spread to other areas of the country. It has therefore always been simply one dialect among many. It is also just as subject to change as any other dialect, and in many cases has 'deviated' much further through linguistic change from older stages of the English language than other varieties.

Attitudes of this type, then, have no foundation in linguistic fact. But we have to recognise that they exist. Letter-writers to newspapers and *The Radio Times* often complain about what they consider to be 'bad English' and the same sort of attitude can be found elsewhere. One College of Education lecturer said of his students: 'My heart sinks when I get students who stand up and say *I done it, I seen it.*' And he went on to say that he thought this represented 'a sloppiness in language'. The same also occurs with accents. The R.P. accent is often characterised as 'good English', 'talking proper' or as 'having a nice voice', whereas certain regional accents are singled out for opprobrium—as 'bad', 'ugly', 'slovenly', 'garbled' and so on. Not many people in this country feel able to claim with any degree of conviction that a Birmingham accent is as *good* as an R.P. accent, or that someone with a London accent speaks as *well* as a B.B.C. news-reader.

These attitudes, I have suggested, have no basis in linguistic fact. There is no linguistic yardstick for evaluating one dialect or accent as better or worse than any other. Where then do these attitudes about 'good' and 'bad' language come from, and why do so many people hold them?

1. Attitudes to language: linguistic or social?

The answer is that attitudes of this type are not linguistic attitudes at all. They are *social* attitudes. Judgements which *appear* to be about language are in fact judgements based on social and cultural values, and have much more to do with the social structure of our community than with language. What happens is that, in any society, different groups of people are evaluated in different ways. Some groups have much more prestige and status than others, and, as a result, dialects and accents associated with these groups tend to be more favourably evaluated than other varieties. Types of language associated with high-prestige social groups are therefore considered 'good' and 'attractive' and so on, while other varieties are evaluated as less good in comparison. Judgements about 'good' and 'bad' language are therefore based on the

28

social connotations of dialects and accents rather than on anything inherent in the linguistic varieties themselves. They are judgements about speakers rather than about speech.

We can attempt to demonstrate this point in the following way. In Chapter 1 we discussed the fact that there is a relationship between language, on the one hand, and regional and social background, on the other. We can now examine the relationship between language and social background in more detail, with the help of results obtained in recent sociolinguistic surveys carried out in Britain and the United States. In the past few years a number of sociolinguistic studies of urban dialects have been undertaken by linguists who have concentrated on obtaining tape-recordings of English as it is actually used and spoken in everyday conversation.

One of the first of these studies was carried out in Detroit, where tape-recordings were made of several hundred speakers who had been selected by random sampling methods and had agreed to co-operate in the recording of interviews. One of the features that the linguists studied in this survey—and it is a feature that is as frequent in British English as in American— was the grammatical phenomenon linguists call *multiple negation*. Take the sentence:

> *There's some milk on the table*

In standard English dialect there are two different ways of making this sentence negative. Either the verb *is* can be made negative by putting a *not* after it:

> *There isn't some milk on the table*

or, more usually:

> *There isn't any milk on the table*

(because of a rule of English grammar which normally changes *some* to *any* in cases like this). Or the *some* can be made negative by changing it to *no*:

> *There's no milk on the table*

The same thing is true of all sentences of this type:

I want none	:	*I don't want any*
It was no good	:	*It wasn't any good*

and so on.

On the other hand, in many non-standard dialects there is also a third possibility. Both types of negation can be carried out simultaneously. The result is:

There isn't no milk on the table
I don't want none
It wasn't no good

This is the grammatical construction often referred to as the 'double negative'. *Multiple negation* is a more accurate label because there is actually no restriction to two negatives. Three or more can be found in sentences like:

I couldn't find none nowhere

Interestingly enough, multiple negation is one of the areas where standard English has deviated further from older stages of the language than many other dialects. At earlier periods, multiple negation occurred in all dialects, and can be found in the English of Chaucer and other writers.

From their tape-recordings the Detroit researchers were able to work out a multiple negation percentage score for each person. This was based on the number of times he used a multiple negative form out of the total number of times he could have used one. The speakers were also assigned to one of four social class groups, ranging from upper middle-class to lower working-class, on the basis of their occupation, education, income, and other factors. Then average multiple negation percentage scores could be calculated for each social class, and the results were as shown in Table I. (Note that these figures do not refer to the percentage in each class who used multiple negation. Most speakers used both forms to varying degrees. The figures refer to the total percentage used on average by one class as a whole.)

TABLE I: % MULTIPLE NEGATIVE FORMS USED IN
DETROIT BY SOCIAL CLASS

upper middle-class	: 2
lower middle-class	: 11
upper working-class	: 38
lower working-class	: 70

It is clear from these figures that there is a strong relationship between usage of this grammatical feature and social class membership. Multiple negation is much more frequent in the speech

30

of members of the lower social class groups than in that of members of the higher classes. (Similar scores would certainly be obtained in most other parts of the English-speaking world.)

It is because there is this clear relationship between grammatical features and social class that we are able to talk about *social class dialects*. Table 1 shows that social class dialects, like regional dialects, form a continuum rather than discrete units. It is not the case that some classes use multiple negation and others do not. It is simply the proportions that are different. The same sort of picture emerges for other grammatical features.

A second example of the relationship between the usage of a grammatical feature and social class can be taken from England. In the standard English dialect the present-tense form of verbs is as follows:

> *I think*
> *you think*   but   *he thinks*
> *we think*
> *they think*

The third-person singular form has an *s* which the other forms do not have. As far as conveying any information is concerned this *s* is quite redundant, and some English dialects no longer have it. They have regularised the present tense to give forms without *s* throughout: *he think; she go; it give*. These dialects include a number in America and, in Britain, dialects spoken in East Anglia. In an urban dialect survey carried out in Norwich this

TABLE 2: % 3RD-PERSON SINGULAR PRESENT VERBS
WITHOUT *s* IN NORWICH

UMC	:	0
LMC	:	29
UWC	:	75
MWC	:	81
LWC	:	97

feature was selected for study. Third-person singular present-tense verb forms without *s*, as opposed to those with, were counted and percentage scores were calculated for individuals and then for social class groups. The results are given in Table 2. This illustrates once again the clear relationship between dialect and social class, with lower-class speakers tending to use many more forms without *s* than higher-class speakers.

With the help of these two examples—and very many others could have been given—we can now begin to explain why the different attitudes displayed towards different English dialects take the form that they do. Many people would say that *I don't want none* and *he love her* are 'bad English', and that *I don't want any* and *he loves her* are 'good English'. We have seen that the adjectives 'good' and 'bad' have no basis in linguistic fact, and can now therefore re-interpret statements of this type in the following way. Members of the higher social classes in our society —people like doctors, top civil servants and bankers—have higher prestige and status than members of lower social class groups—people like dustmen, factory-workers and street-cleaners. This prestige 'rubs off' onto their language. Grammatical features—and dialects in general—that are associated with members of the middle (and especially upper-middle) classes acquire high status. As a result they are considered to be 'good'. On the other hand, features like multiple negation and lack of third-person *s*, as Tables 1 and 2 clearly show, are more typical of working-class speech. As a result of this association, they have low prestige, and are considered to be 'bad'. We can therefore state quite categorically that grammatical forms such as the *I done it* and *I seen it* that our college lecturer believed to be 'slovenly' are not 'bad' or 'corrupt' or 'careless'. Rather, they are grammatical constructions which are typical of lower middle-class and, in particular, working-class dialects and therefore have low social status. This is a very important difference.

2. Social judgements about accents

Exactly the same point should be made about accents. In this country it is widely held to be 'good' to pronounce an *h* in words like *hill* and *hammer*, and 'bad' not to pronounce an *h*. (In fact many people talk of 'dropping' *h*s rather like cricketers talk about dropping catches—as if the *h* ought to be there and its absence is due to carelessness.) These attitudes are again due to the fact that middle-class accents, including R.P., tend to have *h*, whereas many lower-class regional accents do not.

We can demonstrate that there is a close relationship between pronunciation of *h* and social class by taking figures obtained in the Norwich survey, together with similar figures from another

32

urban dialect study carried out in the Bradford area of Yorkshire. Table 3 gives the percentage of possible *h*s pronounced on average by different social class groups in the two areas.

TABLE 3: % *h*s PRONOUNCED

	Bradford	Norwich
UMC	88	94
LMC	72	86
UWC	33	60
MWC	11	40
LWC	7	40

It shows that there is a clear relationship between usage of *h* and social class in both places, and it is interesting to note that not even the highest class consistently uses *h*. (The higher percentage of *h* pronounced in Norwich is partly due to the fact that rural accents in East Anglia are more or less unique in the south of England in preserving *h*, and several of the speakers interviewed in Norwich came from the surrounding rural areas. The loss of *h* in the history of the English language is quite easily explained. Most consonants in English can, like *d*, occur anywhere in a word: before a vowel, *dot*; before certain consonants, *drum*; between two vowels, *ready*; after certain consonants, *wild*; and after a vowel, *red*. Of these five positions, *h* can occur in only one, before a vowel, as in *hill*, *hammer*, *help*, except for a very small number of words like *behind* and *ahead* where it comes between two vowels. This means that it is not a very 'useful' consonant, and one which can be used to distinguish between only a small number of words such as *hill—ill*, *ham—am*, *head—Ed*. In most cases the words involved are unlikely to occur in the same context, and the loss of *h* causes very little confusion, if any at all. It could therefore be claimed that accents without *h* are in a sense more 'efficient' than those with.)

A second example of the way in which accents and social class are related can be taken from a study made in Glasgow. Here one of the features investigated was the pronunciation of *t* between two vowels (as in *better*) or at the end of a word (as in *bet*) as a *glottal stop*. This is the pronunciation that is often indicated in print by writing *better* as *be'er*, and can be heard in many different parts of Britain. (It is often described as 'dropping your *t*s', but this is not an accurate description. The *t is* there—it is simply pronounced as a glottal stop. If the *t* was 'dropped' altogether, speakers who use this pronunciation would make *fleeting*, for example, sound like *fleeing*—which they do not.)

The glottal stop pronunciation of *t* is often thought to be 'bad English', in spite of the fact that the glottal stop is a perfectly normal speech sound used as a consonant in many of the world's languages. The reason for this attitude can be deduced from Table 4, which gives the percentage of glottal stops used by members of different social class groups in Glasgow. The evidence is clear. Pronunciations which are felt to be 'good' are exactly those used most often by higher-class speakers, while features of accent most closely associated with lower-class groups have no prestige and are considered 'bad'—like the glottal stop and lack

TABLE 4: % GLOTTAL STOPS PRONOUNCED. GLASGOW

UMC	:	48
LMC	:	73
UWC	:	84
LWC	:	92

of *h*. As with dialects, when people pass judgement on accents they are not judging the language itself as 'good' or 'bad'. Rather, they are passing comment on the different social connotations that accents and features of pronunciation have.

A very good illustration of this point is provided by differences between American and English accents in the pronunciation of what linguists sometimes call *post-vocalic r*. This is the *r* in words like *car*, where it occurs at the end of a word, and words like *cart*, where it occurs before a consonant. Most accents of English are identical in their treatment of *r* in other positions in the word, as in *rat*, *trap*, *carry*. But they fall into two groups as far as post-vocalic *r* is concerned. Some English accents have post-vocalic *r*—they actually pronounce an *r*-sound in words like *cart* and *car*. These accents include most American, Canadian, Irish and Scottish accents and, in England, accents from the West Country and parts of the North-West and North-East. They are often described as having a 'burr' or as 'rolling the *r*'. Other accents do not have an *r*-sound in words of this type. They include many English English accents, R.P. among them.

If you are not sure if you normally pronounce post-vocalic *r* or not, try saying *mar* and *ma*. If you say these words the same, you do not have post-vocalic *r*. If you make a difference, you do. In

34

accents without post-vocalic r, *cart* does not become the same as *cat*. While the r-sound of *rat* and *carry* cannot be heard in *cart* in these accents, *cat* and *cart* are still distinguished by means of a difference in the vowels. The two vowels are the same as those in *Pam* and *palm* respectively. (This example will probably be help-ful only to people from England and Wales, since many Scottish and Irish speakers have the same vowels in *Pam* and *palm*.)

In England—but not in Ireland or Scotland—accents which pronounce post-vocalic r have lower prestige, other things being equal, than those which do not pronounce it. R.P. does not have post-vocalic r, and in the minds of some people, at least, the pronunciation of this r is associated with speakers who are un-educated or rural, or both. (This stereotype is often, of course, entirely unjustified.) People from places like London are quite liable to find it amusing, and radio comedy shows certainly tend to use it for comic effect. In many parts of America, on the other hand, the situation is completely reversed. In New York, for example, people who do not pronounce an r in *cart* and *car* are often looked down on, and their accent is considered 'bad'. Americans even talk about 'dropping your rs' in the same way that British people talk about *h*s.

There is no better example than this to illustrate the extent to which judgements about 'good' and 'bad' language are, from a linguistic point of view, completely arbitrary, and without founda-tion. There is nothing inherently 'good' or 'bad' about post-vocalic r. It simply has different social connotations in different places. The true explanation for the different attitudes to post-vocalic r in England and America lies in the fact that the rela-tionship between r-pronunciation and social class is diametrically opposed in the two countries. This is illustrated in Table 5. The table gives scores for the percentage of possible post-vocalic rs actually pronounced by speakers recorded in surveys carried out in New York, and in Reading, which is in the West Country r-pronouncing region in England.

TABLE 5: % POST-VOCALIC R PRONOUNCED

	New York	*Reading*
UMC	32	0
LMC	20	28
UWC	12	44
LWC	10	49

3. Aesthetic judgements about accents

Some people may be prepared to accept the point that dialects are evaluated as 'good' or 'bad' because of their social connotations rather than any inherent superiority or inferiority. They may, on the other hand, be much less willing to accept that the same is true of accents. This is because, even if you recognise that all pronunciations are in theory equally 'good', in practice some accents really do appear to sound much 'nicer' than others. Most people find some accents 'pleasant', 'attractive' and 'charming', and others 'harsh', 'ugly' and 'unattractive'. Nearly all of us know accents that we enjoy listening to and others we dislike, and it is therefore not unreasonable to suppose that some types of pronunciation are simply aesthetically more pleasing than others.

However, I want to argue here that judgements of this type about accents are *not* aesthetically based. In fact there is a considerable amount of evidence to demonstrate that there is no inherent 'ugliness' or 'attractiveness' in any accent. On the contrary, evaluations of different accents which are apparently aesthetically based are once again really social judgements. Accents are rated as 'attractive' or 'ugly' because of the social connotations they have.

It is actually rather easy to show that this is so. First, evaluation of accents has quite a lot to do with social class. Few people characterise the R.P. accent as 'ugly', while many of those accents which are so characterised are low-prestige accents associated with the working class. Secondly, it is not a coincidence that most of those accents which are widely held to be 'ugly' are *urban* accents. Places like Birmingham, London, Glasgow, Newcastle, Liverpool and the Potteries are often singled out as having particularly 'harsh' or 'slovenly' accents. Neither is it an accident that many of those accents which are regarded as 'nice'—or at worst 'quaint'—are associated with rural areas, like Devonshire and Highland Scots. In our heavily urbanised society, the rural way of life, and the countryside generally, have pleasant connotations for many of us. Many town dwellers have a nostalgic, romantic attitude to rural areas as representing a peaceful kind of existence which has been lost in the towns. The *connotations* of a rural accent, therefore, are pleasant.

Thirdly, it is also a simple matter to show that you must know what the social connotations of an accent are before you can evaluate it as 'attractive' or 'ugly'. If you dislike Birmingham accents, this is only because you *know* that someone with a Birmingham accent comes from Birmingham, and because you *know* that Birmingham lies at the heart of a heavily industrialised area. The truth of this statement is demonstrated by the fact that foreigners, even including English-speakers such as Americans, not only do not rate Birmingham accents as more 'ugly' than, say, Shropshire accents. In most cases they cannot even hear the difference! The fact is that they do not *recognise* a Birmingham accent and do not know what connotations it has. After all, how many British people can distinguish between more than two or three American accents (or even tell an American accent from a Canadian)—let alone compare them as more or less 'attractive' in the way that Americans do? A Birmingham accent—or any other accent—is not *intrinsically* 'ugly', and nobody unfamiliar with British English accents would tell you that it was. Neither is R.P. inherently 'nice'. It is just that, as many of its speakers are those who are widely considered to be 'cultured', it has come to be regarded as such.

The fact that no accent is aesthetically superior to any other has been demonstrated in a very convincing way by experiments that have been carried out at the University College of Cardiff. In these experiments English-speakers who had little or no knowledge of French were asked to listen to tape-recordings of examples of three different French accents. Previously it had been found that there was a high level of agreement amongst Canadian French-speakers about the merits of the three accents. Educated European French was rated more favourably than educated Canadian French, which in turn was rated more favourably than working-class Canadian French. The English-speakers reacted in a very different way. They did not agree at all as to which accent was the most pleasant, and on average they rated all three accents as the same. In other words, they simply did not find that the 'ugly' French accent was at all unpleasant. For them it was just a sequence of speech sounds with no agreeable or disagreeable connotations.

The educational implications of this should be reasonably clear. Most of us will probably find some children's accents less pleasing than others, but we should recognise these attitudes for what they are, and acknowledge that they have no aesthetic basis. If we do dislike an accent, it is because of a complex of factors that have to do with our own social, political and regional biases rather than with anything aesthetic. We like and dislike accents because of what they *stand for*, not for what they are. We therefore have to be careful not to evaluate children whose accents we like as having greater academic potential or more satisfactory personalities than those whose accents we find unattractive.

4. 'Right' and 'wrong' in language

We have seen, then, that judgements about some varieties being 'better' than others have no basis in fact, and that the same is also true of apparently aesthetic judgements about the relative attractiveness of different accents. Standard English, we have to say, is associated with higher-status speakers in our community and has prestige only for that reason. For many people, in fact, the prestige of standard English is so high that they consider it not only to be 'good', in the way that we have just discussed, but also to be 'correct'. There are many, in other words, who believe that standard English grammatical forms are 'right' and that forms from other dialects are 'wrong'.

I have tried to show that when people say a dialect is 'bad' they are really referring to the dialect's low social status. The same is just as true of notions about 'correctness'. Grammatical features which are regarded as 'correct' are exactly those which are also considered 'good'—because of their social implications. From a purely linguistic point of view, it makes no sense to talk about 'right' and 'wrong' in language. No one would suggest that French is 'more correct' than English, and there is no reason for treating dialects of the same language in anything other than the same way. No one dialect of English is any more 'right' or 'wrong' than any other.

Nevertheless, we have to recognise that many people sincerely believe that certain English constructions and pronunciations are 'wrong'. Let us examine some of the reasons they might put forward in support of their view. First, they could claim that a particular form is a *mistake*. Teachers, for instance, might suggest that if a child were to add 2 + 2 and arrive at the answer 5, they would have to correct his mistake. Surely, they might argue, it is therefore legitimate to correct a child who makes the mistake of saying *I done it* or *He seen it*.

The answer to this argument is that grammatical forms of this type are *not* mistakes. It is quite in order to correct $2 + 2 = 5$ because there is an *inherent truth value* in $2 + 2 = 4$. If two plus two did not make four, the world as we know it would not exist.

38

To get this sum wrong, therefore, is to make a mistake about the very nature of things. The same is very far from being true of grammatical forms like *I done it* and *I ain't got it*. There is no inherent truth value in statements to the effect that 'the past tense of *do* is *did*'. Even if everybody in the whole English-speaking world were to begin to say *I done it*, it would not make any difference to anything important. In fact, it is probably safe to say that a majority of English-speakers normally do say *I done it* already. And this brings us to a further point: if *I done it* is a 'mistake', is it not a rather strange matter when nearly everybody makes exactly the same mistake?

Another argument that people advance in favour of the correctness notion is that *I done it* and *I don't want none* are 'not grammar' or 'bad grammar'. This argument is based on a rather inadequate notion of what grammar is. All dialects of English, as of other languages, 'have grammar', and they are all equally grammatical in the true sense of the word. *Grammar* is a term which, amongst other things, refers to the way in which words are combined into sentences, and to the relationships which hold between sentences. It is also concerned with the functions of different parts of speech, and with restrictions on which combinations of words are possible. Since these are matters which affect them all equally, all dialects must be considered to have grammar. It is simply the case that different dialects of English have different grammars, and slightly different ways of doing particular grammatical operations.

Take, for example, the following difference between most Scottish and most English dialects:

	English	*Scottish*
a.	You went out, didn't you?	You went out, didn't you?
b.	You had a good time, didn't you?	You had a good time, hadn't you?
c.	You had known him for years, hadn't you?	You had known him for years, hadn't you?

The grammars of most dialects spoken in England require you to use the form *didn't* in both sentences *a.* and *b.* while Scottish dialects require this only in the case of sentence *a.* The point is that, in the English dialects, *have* is treated in one way when it operates as a full verb (as it is in sentence *b.*, where it is treated like the full verb *went* in sentence *a.*) and in another when it is used as

39

an auxiliary in the formation of perfect tenses (as in sentence *c.*). In many Scottish dialects it is not. The grammatical structure of the two sets of dialects is different.

Similarly, different dialects have different ways, all equally grammatical, of dealing with relationships between different forms of the same verb. Take some forms of the verb *do*:

	some non-standard dialects	*standard English dialect*
present	you *do* it every day	you *do* it every day
past	you *done* it yesterday	you *did* it yesterday
perfect	you've always *done* it	you've always *done* it
'tag-question' form	you saw him, *did* you?	you saw him, *did* you?

These dialects are all grammatically structured, with rules for converting one form into another, and similar operations. They differ grammatically, in the above examples, only in that the non-standard dialects have identical forms for the *past* and *perfect*, while standard English has identical *past* and *'tag-question'* forms. (The verb *do* is somewhat unusual in English in that it is one of only a small number of verbs that can be used in 'tag-questions'. Others include *have, be* and *can*. The point about grammatical structure holds good, however.) Grammar, then, has to do with the grammatical structure of individual dialects and what grammatical forms each dialect permits.

What, therefore, do people mean when they say that *I done it* is 'not grammar'? They mean that it is a low-status dialect form. But they probably also mean that it is a form that does not appear in what are commonly called 'grammar books'. This is because, traditionally, books with titles like *English Grammar* have been descriptions of the standard English dialect (masquerading of course as grammars of *the* English language). They have also usually been only partial descriptions of the grammar of this dialect since they have concentrated on features (like *I did it*) where many non-standard dialects differ from standard English. This is because the grammars were intended to point out to speakers of non-standard dialects where they were 'going wrong'. (Modern grammars, on the other hand, such as the recent *Grammar of Contemporary English*, concentrate not on what someone thinks people *ought* to say, but on what they *do* say; they specify which dialect they are a description of; and they attempt to provide a grammatical description of the dialect as a whole.) *I done it,* then, *is* 'grammar'—but it is not standard English grammar.

A further argument in favour of the 'correctness' notion might be that people often ask questions like 'which is right, *I saw it* or *I seen it*?' and that they have a right to an answer, if only to put their minds at rest. However, the answer to questions like this should be, as we have seen, 'they are both equally correct'. If this is followed by further questions of the type 'well, which one should I say, then?', then a perfectly respectable answer would be 'it doesn't matter'. But this would be to simplify the issue considerably. In the next two chapters questions of this type will be given further and more sympathetic consideration.

'Correctness' arguments are also often advanced in connection with pronunciation. In particular, we come across arguments of the type 'it must be wrong to say *ammer* because *hammer* is spelt with an *h*'. This argument is also unfounded. We saw in Chapter 1 that writing is primarily a way of recording speech in a relatively permanent way on paper. Speech comes first, writing second. This means that if speech and writing are not in accord it is because the writing system is inadequate, not the speech. For those English-speakers who normally say *ammer* the English spelling system has an inadequate way of representing the pronunciation of this word. There is nothing surprising about this, of course. The English spelling system is notorious for the extent to which it diverges from pronunciation at certain points—although this is not to say that it is quite so chaotic as some people have tried to make out.

Arguments of this type about 'correct' pronunciations are usually rationalisations for sentiments of various kinds against accents with low status. This is demonstrated by the fact that no one suggests that to 'drop' the *h* in *hour* is 'wrong' or 'slovenly', because not even R.P. speakers pronounce the *h* in this word. Neither does anybody claim that the *h* in words like *night, light, thought* and *eight* should be pronounced, and that it is 'wrong' not to do so. In fact some speakers do pronounce the *h* in these words. Many lowland Scots use a pronunciation usually represented on paper as *nicht, thocht*. But their accents do not have high prestige, even though they do 'pronounce the letter *h*'. On the contrary, in Scotland this pronunciation is often looked down on, and certainly has lower status than the more widespread *h*-less pronunciation.

It is also as well to point out that we cannot legitimately talk

41

about 'pronouncing a letter'. Letters are not pronounced, only sounds. If a letter does not represent anything in the pronunciation, like the *h* in *hour* in all accents, and the *h* in *hell* in some, then it is the spelling which is inaccurate, not the pronunciation. ('Inaccurate' is not the same as 'useless': the *h* in *hour* is quite useful sometimes to indicate a difference on paper between *hour* and *our* that cannot be produced in pronunciation.) Strictly speaking it would be more accurate to say, not 'the letter *h* is pronounced such-and-such in English' but 'the sound such-and-such is represented in writing by the letter *h*'.

5. Two types of 'mistake' in English

The notion of 'correctness', although without linguistic justification, is now very pervasive in the English-speaking world, even though it has been current only for three or four centuries. (Before that no one troubled very much about what was 'right' or 'wrong' in English.) In that time, with the help of 'grammar books', this notion has had the effect of stigmatising a number of English grammatical features—features which are quite natural in English but are still felt to be 'incorrect'.

These features fall into two groups. The first group consists of features which are quite natural to all native English-speakers and are clearly part of standard English as well as other dialects, but which many people still feel rather uncomfortable about. One example is sentences which end with a preposition:

I've bought a new car which I'm very pleased with

Sentences of this sort are used all the time by all English-speakers, but there are still people who claim that it is 'wrong' and should be replaced by:

I've bought a new car with which I'm very pleased

The reason for this is rather interesting. During the Middle Ages and for some centuries afterwards the relationship in this country between Latin and English was very like the present-day relationship between standard English and the non-standard dialects. Latin was the language used by the learned, it was the only language widely used in writing, and had high prestige. English, on the other hand, had low status, and was not employed in academic literature. In fact a scientific treatise in English would have been as strange in the mediaeval world as the non-standard

42

English paragraph on anthropology on p. 27 appears to many people today. Latin was therefore considered to be 'good' and English 'bad'. Moreover—and here again there are similarities with the modern situation—the prestige of Latin was often taken even further. At many points where the natural grammar of English differed from that of Latin, Latin was considered to be *right* and English *wrong*. One of these points was the occurrence in English, as in other related languages such as Danish and Swedish, of prepositions at the end of a sentence. Prepositions could not occur at the end of a sentence in Latin, so many people began to feel that they ought not to in English either. To a certain extent this feeling has survived until the present day, with the result that many people still feel that this grammatical construction in English is 'wrong'.

A second example is provided by sentences such as:

It's me!
It was him that did it

These are sentences where the pronouns that are normally used as objects of the verb (*me, him, her, us, them*) occur after forms of the verb *to be*. Many people feel rather uncomfortable about constructions such as these and believe that it is more 'correct' to use the subject forms of pronouns (*I, he, she, we, they*):

It is I!
It was he who did it

Of course, the overwhelming majority of English-speakers always say *It's me*, but the feeling still persists that it is 'better' to say *It is I*. This feeling is also due to the influence of Latin. The grammatical structure of Latin requires that forms of *be* should be accompanied by subject rather than object pronouns. Because of the inferiority complex English writers had *vis-à-vis* Latin, many of them tried to transfer this foreign pattern into their own language, and the Latin rule for pronoun usage even found its way into books on 'English grammar'.

None of these forms can legitimately be described as 'mistakes'. *The car I'm pleased with* and *It's me* are perfectly normal English grammatical forms, and should be regarded as such. It is true that some commentators, while not claiming that *The car I'm pleased with* is wrong, will still suggest that it is 'better style' to write *The car with which I'm pleased*. Judgements about style in this literary sense are a very subjective matter, and it is therefore difficult to comment on statements like this. We can, however, point out that notions about good and bad style are, as far as features like prepositions are concerned, very probably linked to feelings about some forms being more 'correct' than others. This is not, of course, to say that there is no such thing as 'good style' in writing—but merely to point out that our perception of what is stylistically good may be affected by 'correctness' notions.

The second group of stigmatised features in English are rather different. These are features which are quite natural and grammatical in English—but only in some dialects. They are stigmatised simply because they do not occur in standard English. Some of these features are widespread, and are found in many non-standard dialects. In these cases it is often standard English which is the odd man out. Features in this category, some of which we have already discussed, include:

1. Multiple negation: standard English is unusual in not having forms like:

    He didn't want none of it

2. Verb forms: in many cases the past-tense forms of irregular verbs are different in standard English:

    You done it
    He come home yesterday

3. Pronoun apposition: standard English tends not to have forms such as:

    My husband he's asleep in bed

4. The form *ain't*: this corresponds to standard English *aren't, isn't, hasn't, haven't* etc., and occurs with different pronunciations (*ain't, in't, en't* etc.) in different places:

    I ain't done it
    I ain't coming

Other features are regionally more restricted. We have already noted examples such as:

1.   *I wants it* (W. Country and elsewhere)
2.   *He want it* (East Anglia)

Many other examples could be cited including, from different parts of the country:

3. relative pronouns:

    The man what said it
    The man as said it

44

4. demonstratives:

   Them ones over there

5. personal pronouns:

   Us don't like it
   He hurt hisself

6. forms of be:

   You am stupid
   He weren't here
   They wasn't ready

None of these forms are mistakes, either. All we can say about them is that they are grammatical forms that are not found in the standard English dialect and that, for that reason, they tend to have low prestige.

Does this mean, then, that nothing in English is a mistake? Not exactly. People do make mistakes. In writing we can find errors such as the omission of words, spelling mistakes, and, particularly on the part of children, the use of expressions which do not exist (*in results of this*, for example). In speech people can make slips of the tongue, get in a muddle, or say something they did not intend to say. And in both speech and writing people can use a word without really knowing what it means. Foreigners especially also make mistakes. They use words incorrectly, and employ grammatical constructions that do not occur in English. (It is safe to suppose that no native speaker would say *I am knowing it since much years*.) It could also be considered an error if a speaker overtly stated that he was going to speak or write a particular dialect and then used a feature which occurred only in another dialect.

Apart from these cases, however, we have to say that all normal adult native speakers know and therefore use their own dialect of English perfectly. No grammatical form which occurs in any English dialect is an error: with the exception of those instances we have just listed, native speakers do not make mistakes.

3 Linguistic diversity and the school

In recent years a large body of educational research has shown that many working-class children do not do so well at school as middle-class children of equivalent intelligence. This under-achievement of the working-class child is a disturbing pheno-menon, and some educationists have been led to suggest that language may play a part in the development of this and other educational problems. In this chapter we shall examine the nature of linguistic diversity in our schools and discuss what role this diversity may have in the creation of difficulties in education.

Linguistic diversity is certainly an important characteristic of British schools. Some children use the standard English dialect, but most do not, and the extent to which a child's dialect differs from standard English varies according to the region he lives in and the social class of his family and friends. Moreover, few children outside private schools are speakers of R.P. The accents of most children are regional to varying degrees. Most teachers, on the other hand, speak standard English or something close to it, at least at school, and while most of them do not have R.P. accents, their pronunciation is generally only moderately regional. Standard English is in many respects the dialect of the school. It is the variety normally used in writing and reading, and in many schools considerable stress is placed on the 'value' of standard English. And although attitudes to regional accents vary from school to school and teacher to teacher, it often happens that non-regional or moderately regional accents are treated as models of what is desirable.

This means that there is often a conflict between the language of teachers and the school, on the one hand, and the language of many children, on the other. Furthermore, because of the rela-tionship between language and social class, this conflict is usually

46

greater for children from working-class backgrounds than for middle-class children. It would therefore not be too surprising to find that aspects of this conflict were of some importance in the development of certain school problems, particularly those which are most serious in the case of working-class children. It is therefore legitimate to ask: is linguistic diversity a problem in British schools and, if so, what exactly is the nature of the problem?

7. Accents, reading and spelling

First of all, let us examine the diversity of accents in our schools and the educational problems that might be supposed to arise from this. One question that is sometimes asked is: do differences in accents make for difficulties in reading and spelling? To take a specific example: if a child comes from certain parts of the south of England, and is of a certain social class, it is quite probable that he will pronounce pairs of words like the following—which are distinguished in other parts of the country—the same:

our	*are*
power	*pa*
tower	*tar* etc.

Does this mean that he will have more difficulty in distinguishing between words of this type when he encounters them in reading than a child who naturally pronounces them differently? Less importantly, will he have more difficulty in learning to spell them?

The answer is probably 'Yes', particularly so far as spelling is concerned. (With reading, context will normally help to make it clear which word is involved—unless a child is reading mechanically.) But it is important to recognise that this is neither a serious nor an unusual problem. All English-speakers have to face the problem of words which are pronounced the same but spelled differently. We all have to learn that a particular combination of sounds is spelled in one way if it means one thing and in another if it means something else. Pairs of words like the following are spelled differently but pronounced the same by nearly all speakers of English:

meet	:	*meat*
piece	:	*peace*
beer	:	*bier*
past	:	*passed*

$$\begin{array}{ccc} sun & : & son \\ red & : & read \end{array}$$

There is a *general* problem that is common to all accents. However, in the case of other sets of words, there are *particular* problems that vary from region to region. Some accents make a distinction between some sets of words while others do not. For example, most speakers from England pronounce pairs like these the same:

$$\begin{array}{ccc} which & : & witch \\ whales & : & Wales \\ whether & : & weather \end{array}$$

Most Scottish speakers make a difference. But most Scottish speakers make no distinction between pairs like:

$$\begin{array}{ccc} taught & : & tot \\ naughty & : & knotty \\ caught & : & cot \end{array}$$

while most English speakers do. Whether you have spelling (and perhaps reading) problems with *wh/w* or *au/o* therefore depends on where you come from. Many other examples could be given. English orthography, because its relationship with pronunciation is often not particularly close, does not really favour one accent over any other. As a consequence, problems of reading and spelling are *equivalent* for nearly all speakers although they are not actually *identical* in all cases.

Difficulties, however, do occur. The most problematical situation is one where the teacher and child have markedly different accents and the teacher is not aware of the nature or extent of the differences. There is usually, for example, no difficulty in teaching a Scottish child that *caught* and *cot* are written differently. But problems might possibly occur if the teacher is English and does not realise that the child pronounces the two words the same. A teacher in this situation may be unable, at least at first, to appreciate the nature of the child's difficulty.

The sort of problem that can arise through insufficient knowledge or awareness on the part of the teacher is illustrated by an incident that was observed at a junior school in Norwich, involving a student teacher who was not familiar with Norwich accents. People who speak with a Norwich accent make a difference between sets of words which sound the same in most other

48

accents. (The Norwich accent has an extra vowel.) In Norwich English pairs of words like these are distinct:

nose	:	*knows*
moan	:	*mown*
toe	:	*tow*
road	:	*rowed*

As said by a Norwich speaker, the word *rowed* (as in 'he rowed the boat') sounds very similar to the same word as said by, say, a Londoner, but *road* sounds rather like an R.P. speaker saying *rude*.

On the occasion in question, a child had to read aloud the word *road*, and did so quite correctly, in his Norwich accent. The student, however, misinterpreted this and thought he was saying *rude*. She therefore said: 'No, it's not *rude*, it's *road*.' But because of the differences between their accents, the child thought she was saying: 'No, it's not *road*, it's *rowed*.' Confusion all round. If instances of this sort are multiplied, there is a serious danger of the child losing all confidence in his reading ability, and becoming very confused. This is reported to have happened in some cases in the U.S.A. where white teachers are faced with black pupils with radically different accents. In Britain, however, differences are generally regional rather than ethnic, and are usually small enough for a teacher to become aware of them quite quickly. (An exception may be provided by some W. Indian children—see p. 84.)

We can therefore suggest that, if a teacher is sufficiently aware of the possibility of accent differences, problems of this sort will not arise. If an English child, when reading aloud, pronounces *which* the same as *witch*, he is reading correctly. A Scottish (or Irish) teacher sensitive to accent differences will recognise that this is the case, and not interpret this as a misreading. (In fact, attempts by a Scottish teacher to say to an English child: 'No, it's *which*, not *witch*' will only lead to confusion, since the child will almost certainly not notice the difference.) Similarly, if a London child pronounces *our* the same as *are*, he is reading correctly, and his reading should not be 'corrected'.

2. Accents and reading materials

Accent diversity ought also to be taken into consideration in the preparation of reading materials, particularly those of the phonic type, if problems are to be avoided. As an example of materials which have been developed without, in some cases, sufficient attention being paid to accent differences, we can cite those which involve the Initial Teaching Alphabet. The I.T.A. system does permit teachers to prepare, on their own, materials which are suitable for children in their own region. But the printed I.T.A. materials are in many respects most suitable for children with accents of a southern English type.

The principal aim of the I.T.A. is to improve and simplify initial reading by having, for the most part, one symbol for one sound, and only one sound to each symbol—without diverging too far from traditional orthography, which the child will learn to operate with later on. The I.T.A. is without doubt a much simpler system to master than conventional spelling, but the problem is that, as we have already seen, what sounds the same, and therefore will normally have the same I.T.A. symbol, in one area may very well sound different somewhere else.

Many examples could be cited, but we will confine ourselves to a brief list—including those cases we have already discussed above. First, and most serious, there are a number of instances where the printed I.T.A. materials use the same vowel symbol but where certain accents make a difference in pronunciation. (Each word below stands for a whole set of words with the same vowel).

A.   1. *nose* : *knows* etc. Words of this sort are spelled the same in the I.T.A.—nœs—but are different in Norwich and elsewhere. The child will have to learn that two different sounds have the same spelling, œ, only to find, later on, that traditional orthography does make a distinction, usually *o–e* or *oa* as opposed to *ow*.

2. *days* : *daze*   (different in parts of northern England,
    maid : *made*   E. Anglia, S. Wales and elsewhere. I.T.A.
          etc.   mæd in both cases).

3. *wait* : *weight*   (different in parts of Yorkshire, Lanca-
    way : *weigh*   shire, Cheshire and elsewhere. I.T.A.
         etc.   wæt in both cases).

4. *for* : *more*   (different vowels in Scotland and parts of
    nor : *door*   northern England. I.T.A. has or in both
         etc.   cases).

Secondly, there are many cases where the I.T.A. uses different symbols but where a number of accents have the same pronunciation. Here are just a few:

B. 1. *our* : *are* etc. (the same in London and many other places)
       I.T.A. our : ar

    2. *cot* : *caught* etc. (the same in Scotland)
       I.T.A. cot : caut

    3. *cud* : *could* (the same in most of the Midlands and the
     putt : *put* etc. north of England)
       I.T.A. cud : cꙍd

    4. *here* : *hair* (the same in parts of eastern England)
     fear : *fair* etc.
       I.T.A. heer : hær

    5. *do* : *due* (the same in parts of eastern England)
     who : *Hugh* etc.
       I.T.A. dꙍ : due

    6. *your* : *poor* : *for* etc. (the same vowel in much of
      I.T.A. yꙍr : pꙍr : for   southern England)

C. Finally, there are many problems to do with the fact that, even where different accents have the same sets of vowels, particular groups of words may have one vowel in one area and another in another. For example, nearly all English accents make a difference between *full* and *fool*—they have two different vowels here. (This does not apply to many Scottish and North Irish accents.) But words like *book* and *cook* have the same vowel as *fool* and *school* in some parts of the north of England—and therefore should ideally have the same I.T.A. symbol—but the same vowel as *full* and *put* elsewhere.

    Problems of type B and C are probably less serious than those, like the examples in set A, where there is under-differentiation of I.T.A. symbols for some accents. But confusion can still result if numbers of type B and C cases occur in combination. As an illustration, we can cite problems likely to be faced by children with East Anglian accents—problems which are typical of but not identical to those elsewhere. In seven consecutive lines in one I.T.A. reader, for instance, the following seven words occur: *stood, too, roofs, to, go, show, cucumber*. Table 1 shows which of these words are written with which I.T.A. symbol. It will be seen that four different symbols are used. Table 2 again shows the words divided into four groups, but here the division is made according to whether or not the words have the same vowel sound in East Anglian accents. The table shows that here the vowels of *stood* and *roofs* are the same, but different from those of *too* and *cucumber*, which are again the same—and so on.

TABLE 1: I.T.A. SYMBOLS

ω	ധ	œ	ue
stood	roofs	show	cucumber
to	too	go	

TABLE 2: EAST ANGLIAN VOWELS

stood	too	to	show
roofs	cucumber	go	

In both tables there are four sets of words, but there is no connection at all between the I.T.A. sets and the East Anglian sets. Any child with an East Anglian accent will find this particular aspect of the I.T.A. very confusing indeed.

Difficulties of this sort will, of course, not be confined to East Anglia. The differences we have cited above illustrate how, unless accent diversity is taken into consideration, differences and inadequacies can arise. Although the I.T.A. materials do allow for some regional differences, they do not allow for those we have just cited (nor for several others). In some cases a solution to this problem is not entirely clear. In others, such as those where traditional orthography is superior to the I.T.A. (as in the *nose* : *knows* case), it may be easier to find a solution. In any case, we cannot afford to ignore those children who happen not to have southern English accents. The danger is that the preparation of any phonic reading materials—not only the I.T.A.—in ignorance of the many regional accent differences in Britain will lead to confusion for many children. Moreover, the more regional a child's accent is, the more difficulties he is likely to encounter with these reading materials. The working-class child, in other words, is likely to suffer more from inadequately prepared materials of this kind than the middle-class child with a less regional accent.

3. Changing accents: reading

Most teachers today, particularly in infant and junior schools, are happy to encourage their children to continue, for the most part, to use their natural accents. There is still a body of opinion, however, that says that it would be a good idea for some children, at least, to change their accents—and for schools to encourage them to do this.

We have already seen that no one accent is any better than any other. Why then should there be this movement to decrease linguistic diversity? Why should people change their accents? One argument that is often advanced is based on reading and spelling. It is sometimes said that it is a 'bad thing' for children to 'drop their *h*s' because if they do they will find it difficult to distinguish between words like *hill* and *ill* in reading, or to spell words like *hammer*.

This argument fails to recognise that children who normally say *ammer* are not actually faced with an unusual problem—as we have already indicated in our discussion of *our : are* and similar cases. If a child normally says *ammer* and has to learn to read and write *hammer*, then *h* is for him a 'silent letter' (see p. 41) —and English spelling has many 'silent letters'. This child's problem is no different from that of the R.P. speaker who has to learn *hour* and *right*, or from that of any English-speaker faced with words like *debt*, *lamb*, and *hymn*. Changing his accent will not improve his reading. (We cannot say, either, that the R.P. speaker is presented with *fewer* problems of this kind than the child with a local accent. In many instances the reverse may be the case—witness the *nose : knows* and similar examples above.)

4. Changing accents: comprehension

Another argument which is frequently heard, but is equally unsound, is based on comprehension. It is said that certain children must change their accents or they will run the risk of not being understood. Problems of this type, however, are almost always over-estimated. Differences between accents in the British Isles are hardly ever large enough to cause serious comprehension difficulties. It is true that the bigger the differences between two speakers' accents, the more difficult it will be for them to understand one another. A Londoner, for example, will have more difficulty understanding someone from Tyneside than he will someone from, say, Nottingham. But it is never impossible for a Tynesider and a Londoner to converse. We also have to point out that the Tynesider will have just as much difficulty in understanding the Londoner. It is not the case that some accents are

53

inherently more incomprehensible than others. The relative difficulty is simply the result of accent difference. What is difficult for one person may be easily understandable to another.

It is also true that British people enjoy telling stories of the 'I couldn't understand a word he said' variety about people from other parts of the country. But, again, these stories are generally exaggerated. If a Londoner claims that he 'couldn't understand' a Tynesider, it is clear that he does not wish us to believe the same thing as if he were to say that he could not understand Chinese. If a Londoner, or anybody else, makes a statement of this sort, what he really means is that he had more—perhaps much more—difficulty with the Tynesider than he is accustomed to having when listening to speakers of English. He does not mean that communication and understanding were totally impossible.

Many of us have experienced situations where people have not understood us, or where we have found native speakers of other accents of English very difficult to understand, to the point where we have had to ask them to repeat what they said, perhaps several times. But this nearly always happens in brief encounters with strangers, often in places where we have never been before. The differences between British accents are not large enough to cause anything other than short-lived comprehension difficulties. Given a realisation that there are comprehension difficulties; given good will on both sides (evidence suggests that people sometimes do not understand because they do not want to); and given a little time (to enable speakers to get used to one another)—comprehension soon becomes automatic.

There is no argument here, therefore, for changing children's accents in school. Comprehension is a two-way process, and if we find someone's accent difficult to understand, then this is less a reason for him to change his pronunciation than for us to concentrate more closely and get used to his accent as quickly as possible. This is particularly the case since it is much easier for us to become familiar with another accent than for him to change his (see p. 58). In most cases, therefore, the recommendation is for listeners, not speakers, to become more flexible. The only exception is in cases where the speaker is clearly the odd man out—a solitary Tynesider in Manchester, for example. But in this case there is no need for teachers or anybody else to take active steps to do anything about it. If a speaker, after moving to another area, realises that everyone around him is having some difficulty in understanding him, he will change his accent quite rapidly

54

anyway. He will usually do this in an automatic kind of way, without giving it too much thought, simply by adjusting his speech to a certain degree to the accents he hears around him. The process is largely subconscious, and does not require to be taught in schools.

We only have difficulty in understanding accents that we are not used to, and, if we are accustomed to hearing an accent, it causes us no problems. This is what has led some people to suppose that R.P., together with accents like it, is inherently easier to understand than other English accents—which it is not. No one in this country seems to have any difficulty in understanding R.P. But this is not because it is actually clearer or more comprehensible. It is simply because there are R.P. speakers living in most communities and, in particular, because R.P. is heard so frequently on radio and television that everyone has become accustomed to it.

A good illustration of this point is provided by the history of the way in which American accents have been received in Britain. Until the widespread use of sound-recording techniques, most people in Britain had never heard an American accent. As a result, when films with sound-tracks were first imported from the U.S.A. in the 1920s, there were many complaints that audiences could not understand what people on the screen were saying. Today, however, no one complains that American sound-tracks are incomprehensible. In the past few decades we have become very used to hearing, and understanding, American accents.

5. Changing accents: social stigma

A third argument for attempting to change children's accents in school is worthy of more consideration. This argument rests on the fact that certain accents are socially stigmatised. The argument runs: we recognise that all accents are equally good, but society at large does not recognise this, and unless children acquire more statusful accents they will be at a social disadvantage. By not helping children to 'improve' their accents, we are 'keeping them down' and denying them opportunities for upward social mobility.

These motives are obviously laudable, but we do have to consider them very carefully. First, to what extent is it actually true that children will suffer when, say, applying for jobs, if they speak with a low-status accent? This is often assumed to be self-evidently true, and it is obviously a legitimate assumption in some cases. Some advertisements, for instance, do require that the applicant be 'well spoken' (i.e. with an R.P. accent). But there is also evidence to show that this assumption is not nearly so justified as some people have supposed. A recent study carried out in Glasgow has demonstrated that employees and personnel managers are much less concerned about accents than many teachers might think. Comments included the following:

Medical Faculty Administrator: 'I would say as far as a person's accent is concerned we don't give a damn what it is.'

Personnel Manager, National Manufacturing Firm: 'We don't attach a great deal of importance to accent. I think it's wrong.'

Staff Manager, Marketing Firm: 'We don't pay attention to accent as such. Not at all. Unless it's someone from a foreign land who speaks broken English. But as far as the U.K. is concerned, no.'

There were also, of course, those who were concerned about accents. But it is important to note that a *majority* of personnel managers and employers, including even those from banking, accountancy and insurance firms, said that accent was never an important factor in their selection of staff. Even allowing for wishful thinking, this is an important finding.

Secondly, we have to consider the associations and symbolic values that different accents can have. Although there is no necessary connection at all between personality types and accents, most people react as if there were. Because of a complex of connotations, associations and stereotypes, we all acquire notions about what personal characteristics go together with which accents. Most often these stereotypes are unjustified, but they are nevertheless powerful and a factor to be reckoned with.

A series of investigations has recently been carried out which has shown that listeners react differently to a speaker depending on which accent he uses. These experiments have been based on tape-recordings, and have been carried out in such a way that listeners have not been aware that they have actually heard the same speaker twice (using two different accents) rather than two different speakers. The investigations have demonstrated that listeners rate speakers as having more authority and as being more intelligent when they use an R.P. accent than when they use a regional accent. But they have also shown that speakers using regional accents are more favourably evaluated on features such as personal integrity and social attractiveness (factors such as friendliness, kindness, and so on).

A particularly important experiment along the same lines involved tape-recordings of an argument against capital punishment recorded by the same speaker using both R.P. and regional accents. The results showed that those listeners who heard the R.P. version of the argument evaluated it more favourably than those who heard the regional accent versions. In other words, the quality of the argument was rated as higher when it was spoken in R.P. than when it was spoken in a regional accent. But the experiment also measured how effective the argument actually was by investigating how many listeners changed their minds after being exposed to it. Here it emerged that the regionally accented versions of the argument were much more successful. So, while listeners stated that the R.P. argument was better, it was actually the regional accents that were more persuasive and convincing.

We have to conclude that it is by no means always a social disadvantage to have a regional accent. People who are contemplating losing some of the regional features in their pronunciation ought perhaps to consider whether they think it more important to be persuasive and to be regarded as having integrity and social attractiveness, or whether they would prefer to be thought of as having intelligence and authority.

6. Leaving accents alone

There are also very good reasons for arguing that attempts should *not* be made to change children's accents. We will go into more detail with this argument in Chapter 4, when we come to discuss changing dialects, but we can point out here that one excellent reason for not trying to change children's accents in school is that it will probably not succeed. It is a very difficult if not impossible undertaking. It may be a good idea to point out to children that some accents have more prestige than others, although most children are probably fairly aware of this already. It is a rather different matter to actively encourage children to alter their accents. There are two factors to take into account. First, accents are an important factor in group membership and an important way of signalling group solidarity. Your accent is something you share with those who are like you and with whom you identify. (This is why children have accents like their friends rather than their parents or teachers.) Your accent is also clearly linked to your conception of your own identity. A child, therefore, will not want to change his accent unless he also wants to reject the social group to which he belongs or unless he wants to change his identity in some way. By rejecting a child's accent, or even some features of it, we run the risk of his feeling that we are rejecting *him*. It is therefore dangerous, psychologically and educationally, to attempt to change accents. If we do this, we may well alienate the child from the school (or from his friends and family).

Secondly, to ask a child to change his accent is to ask him to do something very difficult—even ignoring the social and emotional factors that we have just mentioned. Every speaker's pronunciation depends on a very complicated set of neurological and muscular operations which are learnt early on in life and which soon become deeply automatic. To change habits of this type, particularly when this has to be done consciously and artificially in the classroom, is a very difficult task, which is why most people have a 'foreign accent' when they learn to speak a new language. It is true that many people do change their accents, but it is legitimate to ask: at what psychological cost? Because of the difficulty of the task, to change your accent consistently and consciously means that you have to pay far more attention than normal to *how* you are saying things and, consequently, less attention to *what* you are saying. Psychological research recently carried out in Norway suggests that many people who do change their accents are at a considerable psychological disadvantage as compared to those who are able to express themselves in their own accent, without devoting any of their attention to altering automatic pronunciation processes (see also p. 79).

We conclude that children should not be asked to change or even modify their accents. Attempts to do this in school, whether through ridicule or more sympathetic methods, involve a serious danger of alienating the child from the teacher and the school, and are almost certain to fail because of the socio-psychological factors and other difficulties involved. If anyone, later in life, feels the need, for reasons of geographical or social mobility, to change their accent, they will be able to do this with a reasonable degree of success without formal instruction, simply through association with others who have the desired accents. This is a less conscious and, because of the continued reinforcement from others, much easier process than change in the classroom. Even in this case, however, psychological problems are likely to arise, as we have seen.

Educational problems, then, do not arise from variation in

accents, except in those cases where teachers of reading are unaware of differences between their accents and those of their children, or where teachers attempt to change or modify children's accents.

7. Dialect diversity in the school

We must now, therefore, look to diversity in dialects to see if grammatical differences play any part in bringing about educational difficulties. Given that standard English is in many ways the school dialect, it would not be surprising to discover that differences between standard English and many children's speech gave rise to problems. Working-class children, to a greater extent than middle-class children, speak dialects different from standard English. It may well be, therefore, that working-class children have greater linguistic difficulties in school than middle-class children, and therefore lag behind academically.

The following examples have been taken from the written work of children at a junior school in a working-class area. (The spelling has been normalised in one or two cases.)

When I done that I came back in the room.
We was going to build it up again.
I goes up the park every day.
Them men was two bank robbers.
I was playing on me bike.
I see it on television last night.
I run in my mum's room and slept there.
Then we come back and went home.
No one loved him no more.
One day he never gave the girl any pears.

In their writing, these children are simply using forms, from their own dialects, that come naturally to them. The forms are not inferior to standard English grammatical forms, and they are not wrong. In what sense, then, can they be considered to be an educational problem?

The answer appears to be that they are a problem simply because they are not standard English, and can therefore cause difficulties, particularly for working-class children, in two different ways. First, dialect forms such as those we have just cited will represent a problem for any child using them, and in particular writing them, in situations where standard English is expected or regarded as necessary—and therefore rewarded.

(Difficulties will be particularly serious in cases where teachers are unfamiliar with local dialect forms and therefore fail to appreciate why a child has written what he has. However, even where teachers do recognise the source of non-standard grammatical forms, children will continue to use them.) Children who normally speak standard English or a dialect close to it will therefore have an advantage over those who do not, to the extent that the use of standard English by children is regarded favourably. We shall discuss what to do about problems of this nature in Chapter 4.

Secondly, problems can arise as the result of attitudes which may be expressed in school to dialect forms like those we have cited. Problems connected with attitudinal factors are in fact common to both dialects and accents, and we shall discuss them together in the next section.

8. Attitudes to language in school

Because of the relationship which exists between language and social class (and other sociological factors), language can be socially very symbolic. People therefore have attitudes towards different varieties of language which, as we have seen, may be expressed in terms of labels such as 'good', 'correct' and 'pleasant'. Ultimately, however, attitudes of this kind have to do with the connotations, which may be cultural, social, political, regional, racial and so on, that different varieties have.

In school, attitudes to language can be very important. Some children, for example, may find the teacher's language alien in some way, and come to resent the social gulf between them that the linguistic differences symbolise. Children may, usually in a subconscious fashion, find a teacher's dialect 'snobbish' or 'posh', and react to the teacher accordingly. There is little one can do about this linguistically. One simply has to reduce the gulf in other ways, and hope that a good relationship with the child will minimise the effects of his attitudes. Teachers should certainly not attempt to change their own grammatical forms or pronunciation towards those of the child. Unless the teacher is genuinely bi-dialectal, attempts to do this will usually be unsuccessful, and may be interpreted as insincere and insulting by the children. (Vocabulary, of course, is a different matter.)

A more important aspect of this problem, however, is that which involves the attitudes of teachers to the language of child-

60

ren. We must expect all teachers to have attitudes towards different types of language. Everybody in our community has attitudes of this sort. We are all prepared to use adjectives of the type 'affected', 'posh', 'snobbish', 'stilted', 'ugly', 'careless', 'vulgar', 'slovenly' about other people's language, in a denigrating way. Teachers' attitudes are often simply a reflection of those current in the community at large. Sometimes, however, teachers' attitudes may be more strongly held than those of others in the community. Some teachers regard themselves as custodians of what is 'right' in the English language. Other teachers recognise that some people outside the school regard them in this way, even if they do not themselves. And others feel linguistically insecure about their own language, because this 'custodial' role conflicts, they feel, with the low-prestige varieties they once spoke themselves—and they therefore over-react against children's low-status varieties. In any case, strongly felt or not, teachers' attitudes to children's language can be very influential in shaping relationships between the child and the school, and in affecting a child's attitude to education generally.

In the Glasgow survey that we have already discussed, a sample of 48 teachers were interviewed about their attitudes to their children's speech—and other sources suggest that we can accept their attitudes as typical of those teachers in the country as a whole. It emerged that about half the sample believed that schools should not attempt to change children's native dialects, or at least their accents. A typical comment from this group was:

> 'As long as people are articulate, as long as they know what they're trying to say, it doesn't matter what sort of accent they use.'

This is very much the sort of argument that I am trying to put forward in this book, and I want to suggest that teachers with this kind of view are more likely, other things being equal, to establish good relations with their children than those who have more hostile reactions to their children's speech.

Other teachers in the sample were in favour of changing children's dialects and accents. This was usually because they believed that the children's speech was defective, wrong or unpleasant in some way. These teachers criticised dialect features such as 'I done it' and 'I seen it', and made comments such as 'grammatical structure is poor'. We have already seen that statements like this are without foundation.

As far as accents were concerned, some teachers wanted to encourage change because they believed there were 'basic defects' in their children's Glaswegian pronunciation, such as 'the glottal stop, the tendency to run words together, the narrow range of vowel sounds'. Arguments of this nature are misinformed. We have already noted that the glottal stop is a perfectly normal consonant that is in no way a defect. The 'tendency to run words together' is rather more difficult to discuss, as it is not entirely clear what exactly this means. But it suggests that the person who made this comment believes that 'good' speakers pronounce each word separately. In fact there is no support for this belief whatsoever. No speaker of any of the world's languages does this. There are no gaps between words in speech as there are in writing. 'Running words together' is something that all adult native speakers do, and they do it in a very skilful way. When a child begins to be able to do this, it shows that he has mastered the complex rules that govern the production of fluent, natural speech. If you hear someone speaking English who does not 'run words together', it is certain that he is either a very young child, or a foreigner who is having difficulty with English pronunciation. Comments like this are therefore probably the result of the fact that the teacher's accent is different from the child's. This may make for certain difficulties in comprehension, which the teacher then puts down to the child's 'running words together'. There is support for this interpretation when we consider that similar comments occur in other contexts. British people who know a little French sometimes say that it is difficult to understand French speakers because they 'run words together' although French-speakers are no different from English-speakers in this respect.

As far as the 'narrow range of vowel sounds' is concerned, all we can say is that Glaswegian accents have just as many vowel sounds as other English accents—and more than some of them.

Attitudes of this type are due to a lack of information about the nature of language. They can therefore be adjusted by making more information about language available to people involved in education. This is important, because these attitudes and others like them are not only misinformed, they are also unfortunate. If a teacher communicates attitudes of this sort to children, overtly or indirectly, they will soon develop strong feelings of linguistic insecurity. This in turn can result in a child becoming unwilling to speak, inarticulate, hesitant, and resentful. If a child feels his language is inferior, he is less likely to be willing to use it.

It was also clear from the survey that linguistic attitudes of this kind extended to the College of Education level. One lecturer commented:

'I do resent careless speech, where they're clipping word endings and drawing out vowels. I expect from every student, correct speech, a good standard of speech.'

This sort of inaccurate and unjustified statement about other speakers' accents will not, if directed to students, help to establish good relationships with the lecturer. More importantly, though, it will undermine students' confidence in their language and help to implant feelings of linguistic insecurity in the next generation of school-teachers. This is undesirable, since teachers, as much as children, should be thinking about what they are saying, and not how they are pronouncing it.

We can now see, then, that there is another possible educational problem connected with linguistic diversity. Not least of a child's difficulties may be to be told that his dialect and/or accent are 'wrong', 'bad', 'careless', 'sloppy', 'slovenly', 'vulgar', or 'gibberish'—and these are all terms actually observed to have been used in classroom situations. There is also a danger that teachers who have unfavourable attitudes towards low-status varieties may come—unwittingly—to evaluate children who use standard English and high-prestige accents more favourably than children who do not. It has been shown that some teachers regard children who speak and write high-status varieties—and these are usually middle-class children—as having more academic potential, simply because of their language. This could be one factor in the promotion of underachievement on the part of working-class children, since teachers' expectation can be important in influencing a child's academic performance. We cannot expect teachers, any more than anybody else, to change their attitudes overnight, but teachers can be encouraged to become aware of their own attitudes, to make allowances for them, and to recognise the problems they may cause.

9. Summary

Linguistic diversity in schools is or may be a factor in causing educational problems of the following type:

1. Accent: reading and spelling difficulties, if the teacher is not familiar with the child's accent.

63

2. Accent: alienation from school, if attempts are made to change the child's accent.
3. Dialect: interference from the native dialect in standard English, if standard English is required or rewarded.
4. Attitudes: resentment, alienation and linguistic insecurity, if the child's accent and dialect are belittled.
5. Attitudes: subconscious evaluation by the teacher of children with higher-status accents and dialects as academically more promising.

Problems 1, 2, 4 and 5 can be overcome relatively easily, particularly if potential problems and their solutions are discussed in Colleges and Institutes of Education. Problems 1 and 5 will not occur where a teacher's attention is drawn to the possible difficulties, and problems 2 and 4 can be avoided by encouraging teachers to adopt favourable attitudes to their children's language. But what of problem 3? This problem occurs 'if standard English is required or rewarded'. In Chapter 4 we shall discuss to what extent standard English is and ought to be required, and what we can do about it.

4 Why standard English?

We have seen that dialect differences in British schools do not constitute an educational problem *unless* standard English is required of children who have some non-standard variety as their native dialect. In this chapter we shall consider some of the arguments for and against making it a requirement that children should use standard English in this way. The problem is this: should we continue to teach (and reward) the use of standard English in schools, and attempt to solve the difficulties caused by non-standard dialects as best we can? Or should we allow children to speak and write those grammatical forms which come most naturally to them, and thereby avoid giving an advantage to those who already speak standard English? This question is not an easy one to answer. We can, however, begin to tackle it in the following way: if we look back over the years since education became widespread in the English-speaking world, it is possible to distinguish three different approaches that have been adopted to the problem of non-standard dialects in school. We can evaluate these three approaches, and, in weighing up the advantages and disadvantages of each, attempt to decide what are the best courses of action to adopt.

1. Elimination of non-standard English

The earliest and, in some parts of the English-speaking world, still most popular approach to the problem can perhaps be labelled 'the elimination of non-standard English'. People who subscribe to this view, whether they do so consciously or not, feel that the best way to solve the dialect conflict problem is simply to get rid of all non-standard dialects. They believe that some children suffer because they do not speak standard English, and

65

that non-standard dialects are 'incorrect' or 'bad' English. 'Bad English', they feel, should therefore be eradicated.

Now we have already said that attitudes of this type have no basis in linguistic fact. It is not legitimate to suggest that there is anything 'wrong' with non-standard dialects. Rather, we have to say that it is this approach itself which is wrong. And it is wrong not only because it is based on a linguistic misapprehension. It is also wrong because it is impracticable and educationally dangerous.

It is, in the first place, impracticable because it does not and will not work. Generations of teachers have employed persuasion, exhortation, punishment, scorn and ridicule in attempts to prevent children from using non-standard dialects—all of them without success. And there is no reason to suppose that they will be any more successful in the future. There are a number of reasons why this is so. First, to change your dialect, particularly through conscious effort, is a very difficult task (and one we shall discuss further below), so that even if all speakers were determined to speak standard English, this would be an almost impossible situation to arrive at. But the fact is, secondly, that most people do not want to change their dialect. Of course, if you ask many people if they would like to change the way they speak, they will tell you that, yes, they would like to speak 'better'. But if you press them, and ask them if they would *really* like to speak differently, and what would happen if they did, then it emerges that the desire to speak 'better' is really only a very superficial one. Deep down, most people have no desire at all to alter their dialect. If they did make radical changes in the way they spoke, their friends and family would feel that this was disloyal, unnatural and probably ridiculous. And speakers themselves would feel that they were being untrue to their background, way of life, and personality. They would, in short, feel uncomfortable and out of place. The fact is that we all, quite naturally, speak like the people we know best and associate with and value the most— just as we behave, think and dress like them to a considerable extent. Because language is very important as a social symbol in this way, people are very unlikely to change their dialect unless they also change their friends, associates and milieu.

This is particularly true of children. Children do not speak like their parents, and they certainly do not speak like their teachers. They speak like their friends. This is especially noticeable with accents: Scottish parents who move to England, for example, will have children with English accents—and vice versa. But it is

66

just as true of dialects. The most important influence in determining what dialect a school-age child uses is his peer-group. For a child to change his dialect is to isolate himself from his group, and it is an unusual child who will want to do that. There is therefore no hope that non-standard dialects will just disappear from schools. Moreover, in many cases attempted intervention by teachers in matters of dialect may even have an effect the reverse of that intended.

The 'elimination' approach is also dangerous, because it involves making it plain to a child, whether overtly or indirectly, that his language is 'wrong' or 'inferior'. It is difficult to belittle a speaker's language without belittling the speaker as well, and to suggest to a child that he should (although it is of course never put quite like this) change his dialect, because the one he has is no good, is insulting and likely to cause resentment. This is not least because language is a very personal thing—a part of oneself. But it is also because language can be, as we have seen, socially symbolic, so that to reject a speaker's language is to appear to reject not just him, but also all those like him who he identifies with and values. By saying, in effect, 'my dialect is better than yours, so you ought to speak like me', a teacher runs the risk not only of destroying his relationship with the child, but also of alienating the child from school altogether.

There is in particular the danger that, if standard English is held up as a superior dialect which ought to replace the child's own, the child will come to resent and reject anything that has to do with standard English—especially reading. Illiteracy is, of course, a large and complex problem which we can do no more than touch on here. But there is evidence to suggest that some children at least may not learn to read because they do not want to: and that they do not want to for reasons that have to do with group identity and cultural conflict, in both of which dialect certainly plays a role. In Harlem, New York, for instance, it has been shown that it is precisely those boys who are intelligent, well adjusted and well integrated who are the worst readers. It is normal not to read well. This is all part of a pattern of cultural conflict where school and reading form only a portion of the middle-class values that are being rejected. But there is no doubt that the invidious comparison of 'good' standard English with 'bad' non-standard (and, in Harlem, Black) English serves only to heighten the conflict and perhaps to increase opposition to reading, some of which might have been avoided.

The 'elimination' approach is also dangerous in that it usually succeeds in producing in children what I have termed above *linguistic insecurity*. If you tell a child often enough that his dialect is 'wrong' you will not succeed in getting him to change it, but you almost certainly will succeed in making him very unsure about his language. He will not be encouraged to speak a new dialect. He will simply be discouraged from speaking at all. As we have said, years of the 'elimination' approach have not succeeded in doing any eliminating. But they have, unfortunately, succeeded in convincing a majority of the nation's inhabitants that they 'can't speak English'.

When I was making a study of the way English is spoken in Norwich, at least half the people I spoke to and tape-recorded expressed surprise that I should want to talk to *them*. They would say things like 'I'm a very poor talker'; 'I know I speak horrible'; 'I can't speak English properly'. This was particularly sad because most of them then proceeded to give a very convincing demonstration of the fact that they could speak English not only fluently (which is only what one would expect from a native speaker after all) but also vividly, clearly, entertainingly and in a highly skilful manner. (There is nothing unusual about Norwich people in this, of course. My experience has been shared by many others in other parts of the country.)

If many people hold views like this about the value of their own dialects, it is not surprising if some of them, both adults and children, become hesitant and inarticulate when required to speak in certain circumstances. They are reluctant to say anything lest they reveal their 'inability' to speak the language. We can probably agree that one of the tasks of the school is to give children confidence in their ability to use language. This they will not have if they are required to direct half their attention to *how* they are saying things—in case they make a 'mistake'— rather than to *what* they are saying.

2. Bi-dialectalism

A second approach to the dialect conflict problem which has been receiving increasing attention from linguists and others, particularly in the U.S.A., has been labelled 'bi-dialectalism'. This approach recognises that both the standard English dialect and the child's native dialect are valid and good linguistic varieties worthy of attention; and both are considered to be

68

'correct'. The two are treated as separate varieties (even though in many cases there is really a continuum rather than a separation) and are given names, such as 'book language' versus 'local language', decided on by the teacher. The differences between the two dialects are pointed out and discussed as an interesting fact—children do appear to find this sort of thing interesting. And non-standard dialect speakers can then be taught how to convert their own dialect forms into the standard dialect when this is required. The important thing about this approach is that it respects the child's dialect and his feelings about it, and does not try to eradicate or even alter it. It attempts to give the child competence in another dialect—standard English—*in addition to* the one he already has. As a result, there is a much smaller likelihood of bringing about alienation or linguistic insecurity.

It is perhaps only fair to say that, although many linguists have been enthusiastic about this approach, some of them do have a vested interest in it, in that they are sometimes called on —and given money—to devise programmes for carrying out teaching of this sort. In particular, they may be asked to list points of difference between non-standard dialects and standard English so that teachers unfamiliar with the local variety know what contrasts to look out for. (We evaluate the bi-dialectalism approach below.)

3. Appreciation of dialect differences

The third approach, which is the most recent of all, and which again has its most notable advocates in the U.S.A., can perhaps be termed 'the appreciation of dialect differences' approach. Those who subscribe to this view say that, if working-class children and others suffer because of people's attitudes to low-prestige dialects, then the solution is not to change the dialects but to change the attitudes. We should, they say, not waste time trying to teach children to use standard English. Rather, we should attempt to educate people to the view that all dialects are equally good, and that there are no grounds for discriminating against speakers who use non-standard dialects. What we should aim for is a society free from dialect prejudice, where everybody can use their own dialect without fear of ridicule or correction.

Critics of this approach say that it is hopelessly utopian because people's attitudes to low-status dialects are so deeply ingrained that they will never change. In the long run, however, it is likely that this approach will be the most profitable one to adopt. People can be educated, in schools, colleges and elsewhere, to lose their prejudices about dialect, just as prejudices of other sorts have been lost or weakened. In fact, to change the way people think will probably, given time, be much easier than changing the way they speak. There is also the following point to bear in mind. Even if it were possible to change the way people spoke so that everyone used standard English, in any large community small linguistic differences between some social groups would certainly remain, or reappear in time, which those who were so inclined would still be able to seize upon and stigmatise. If groups of people are prejudiced against other groups, they will probably always be able to find linguistic differences to support their prejudices.

Changes of attitude will not only have to take place in the school, of course. Many teachers have found that, however often they try to persuade their pupils that their accents and dialects are good and valuable, the children may still find this hard to accept, simply because of the attitudes they encounter *outside* the school, from parents and others. But school is a good place to start. And those who would like to move towards a situation where all dialects are regarded as equally good should be encouraged by changes that have already taken place. Attitudes to accents in Britain, for example, are very different today from what they were, say, thirty years ago. The B.B.C., for instance, now employs announcers and news-readers with slightly regional accents, something that would have been unthinkable before the war. There is no reason why similar developments should not take place with dialects, particularly since there is already evidence that different groups of speakers are now beginning to change their attitudes to their *own* dialects. American Blacks, for example, are beginning to react more favourably to 'Black English', and French Canadians appear to be losing some of their inferiority complex about European French. The 'appreciation' approach, we can argue, is therefore by no means a hopeless one.

We can conclude, then, that the 'elimination of non-standard English' approach is wrong and to be avoided at all costs. We can also conclude that the 'appreciation of dialect differences' approach is good, hopeful and to be encouraged. But what of the bi-dialectalism approach? In the rest of this chapter I want to attend to the following question: we advocate that the 'appreciation of dialect differences' approach should be followed in schools (in staff-rooms as well as classrooms); but are there any grounds for suggesting that the bi-dialectalism approach should *also* be employed? In other words, are there any reasons why we should continue to teach standard English in schools, by means of the bi-dialectalism method, at the same time as trying to cultivate dialect tolerance? Let us consider some of the reasons that might be put forward for continuing to teach the standard English dialect to British children.

4. Correctness

One argument that we shall doubtless encounter is that standard English is 'correct English', and that it is therefore essential to teach standard English to those who do not use it 'properly', in order to maintain standards. If we permit children to use what-ever grammatical forms come most naturally to them, 'errors' will multiply and 'corruption' of the language will ensue.

We have already discussed and dismissed arguments of this type earlier on. The fact is that there is no such thing as 'correct English', and that notions such as 'corruption' have no part to play in discussions about language. 'Standards' will not fall if we encourage the use and tolerance of non-standard dialects. On the contrary, standards of literacy and articulateness might very well improve.

5. Expressiveness

A second argument that is sometimes used in favour of teaching standard English is that, even if it is not more 'correct' than other dialects, it *is* more expressive.

I have already tried to show (p. 26) that there is nothing you can do or say in one dialect that you cannot do or say in another. There is, that is, no justification at all for claiming that one dialect is any more expressive than any other. There may be a connection between expressiveness and vocabulary, but, as we have already seen, vocabulary is in principle independent of grammatical forms and constructions.

6. Logic

A further argument is that standard English is in some way more logical than other dialects. This argument is usually linked to the appearance in low-status dialects of the phenomenon of multiple negation (see p. 29). We have already stated that there are no reasons for supposing that there is anything wrong with constructions such as:

I don't want none.

But some people have tried to argue that multiple negation is illogical because 'two negatives make a positive', rather as if English were some kind of algebraic system. We can hear arguments like 'if you say you *don't* want *none*, you must mean you *do* want *some*'.

There are several reasons why this is not a valid argument. First, languages are not logical systems. They are linguistic systems. There are many ways in which languages are not 'logical' in this sense: all natural languages incorporate redundancies, repetitions and irregularities. They should not therefore be treated as if they had some kind of rigidly mathematical or logical basis. It is precisely because natural languages are not 'logical' in this way that logicians have had to develop systems of their own.

(Incidentally, if 'two negatives make a positive', presumably 'three negatives make a negative'. This would mean that a sentence like

I can't find none nowhere

is quite 'logical'. But of course opposition to sentences like this is just as strong as opposition to those with only two negatives.)

Secondly, sentences like *I don't want none* (with normal stress and intonation) are never misunderstood by listeners to mean that the speaker does want some. The listener, that is, finds the statement in no way illogical or contradictory, any more than the speaker does. Comprehension difficulties never arise. Even people who are firm believers in the principle that 'two negatives make a positive' can be observed to walk out of shops on being told 'we ain't got none'.

Thirdly, it is worth noting that many of the world's languages not only permit multiple negation (like most English dialects) they actually require it. In Serbo-Croat, the most widely spoken Yugoslavian language, for example, all words that have negative forms *must* be negative in a negative sentence. Thus:

I never saw anybody anywhere

has to be translated as:

Nikad nisam video nikoga nigde

literally:

'Never I-didn't see nobody nowhere.'

Out of the five words in this sentence, four are negative—and they have to be to make it a grammatical sentence in Serbo-Croat.

Standard English, then, cannot be claimed to be any more, or any less, logical than any other dialect.

7. Educational progress

A further argument that we might encounter is that standard English plays a central part in many school activities that are connected with language, and that it is therefore necessary to teach children this dialect so that they can make progress educationally. Certainly, most teachers would agree that children should be able to understand English when they *hear* it; *read* it well; and use it well in *speaking* and *writing*. But how far do these four linguistic activities actually require that children should be taught and encouraged to use *standard* English as opposed to any other dialect? Let us consider the four activities in turn.

8. Hearing and understanding

It is possible to suggest that children need to be taught standard English because they have to be able to understand it when they hear it. Children hear standard English from teachers, as well as from other sources such as radio and television, and it is essential that they should have no comprehension problems when they encounter this dialect.

This argument, in fact, has no validity. In the first place, the grammatical differences between standard English and other dialects, while socially perhaps very significant, are linguistically generally rather small. Even with those varieties most different from the standard dialect—some rural Scottish varieties, for example—there are not enough dissimilarities for serious comprehension difficulties to arise.

Another factor is that all British people, even including young children, are now very familiar with standard English, precisely because they do hear so much of it from radio, television and other sources. For most people, it is far from being a strange dialect, so that even if large linguistic differences *were* involved, they would still have no difficulties in understanding standard English.

Finally, hearing and understanding is, relatively speaking, a passive skill. Just as it is much simpler to learn to understand a foreign language than to speak it, so it is much easier to understand another dialect than to learn to actually use it oneself. British speakers understand American English without being able to speak it, for instance. There is therefore no need whatsoever for children to be taught standard English before they will be able to understand it. No child who does not have some kind of hearing or other impairment should have any comprehension problems with standard English.

(An important exception to this point may be provided by some children of West Indian origin, who may have some problems with understanding standard English when they hear it, as a result of dialect differences. But this is true, for them, of *all* dialects of British English, not just standard English. We discuss the special case of some West Indian children below.)

9. Reading

A further argument might be that children have to learn to read standard English, and that they need to be taught it for this reason.

It is certainly true that children have to learn to read standard English. Nearly everything that is printed in English appears in this dialect. And all introductory reading materials are in standard English, apart from occasional passages of dialogue involving non-standard dialect-speaking characters.

Once again, though, reading is a relatively passive skill. This means that no active ability in a particular dialect is required before one can read it. There are many British people who can read French without difficulty but who speak it very badly. In the same way, children learn to read standard English without actually using it themselves. Many children learning to read do have to cope with a new and different dialect in addition to the task of acquiring proficiency in reading. But the nature of dialect differences in Britain, as we have said before, is not such as to cause any great difficulties, particularly if the teacher is aware of the differences involved and is therefore prepared for any slight problems that might occur.

74

In America, some reading materials for Black children have been prepared, experimentally, in Negro dialect, in an attempt to ease the burden of initial reading by removing the dialect difference factor. (Similar materials have also been prepared for some Swedish and Norwegian children.) In England, dialect differences are relatively so small that materials of this type, in non-standard dialects, would probably give no actual reading advantage. Reading materials specially prepared for Scottish children, on the other hand, might well be beneficial, because of the greater linguistic differences from standard English. And in all parts of Britain materials of this type might be psychologically advantageous. The social distance between the child and the characters he reads about, symbolised by the language differences involved, would be smaller for most children if non-standard dialects were used—which might result in keener readers who were more able to identify with the characters, and thus with the activity of reading itself. The cause of 'appreciation of dialect differences' might also be advanced.

One modern British reading scheme which has attempted to minimise psychological distance in this sort of way—and very successfully—is the *Nipper* series. These books employ non-standard *dialect* forms only in dialogue passages, but they are written in a *style* which is very similar to that used by children in their everyday speech. In other words, care is taken, as in certain other recent reading schemes, not to employ vocabulary or grammatical constructions from formal or artificial styles which children will find very alien. This, of course, was a failing of many earlier readers which tended to employ language that was not only strange to children but often not found in the normal spoken or even written language of adults either. English-speakers, for example, do not normally say 'Come, John, come!' or 'See the dog, John!'

It appears, though, that most British children, when faced with a passage of standard English to read, are rather good at 'translating' it into their own dialect as they go along. Fluent readers, adults and children alike, do not simply register what is on the printed page as they read. They also make predictions about what is coming next. This is why it is very easy to miss printing errors when proof-reading, for example. The reader supplies what ought to be there, even when it is not. In the same way a child, when reading aloud, may supply something that does not actually appear on the page if it is predicted according to the rules of his own dialect. For example, children who speak dialects where present-tense verb forms have an -*s* suffix for all persons may often, when faced with a sentence such as:

They always walk home

produce:

They always walks home.

This 'translation' should not be regarded as a reading error. On the contrary, it is a successful reading in that the child has understood exactly what is being said and has, rather skilfully, converted the printed word into forms that are grammatical in his own dialect. 'Translation' cannot take place, of course, *unless* the child has understood—and should therefore be allowed to pass. In some cases, though, it may be necessary, if a child becomes aware of a discrepancy between what is written and what he has read, to discuss specific differences in order to explain apparently 'extra' or 'missing' letters, or differences in grammatical forms.

Schoolchildren, then, do have to learn to read standard English, but this does not mean that we also have to teach it to them or require them to use it actively.

10. Speaking

Another argument we have to consider is that standard English ought to be taught in schools so that children can learn to speak it. We stated above that one of the school's objectives is to encourage children to use English well in speaking—but *speaking well* has of course nothing to do with which dialect a speaker happens to use. Most people, in fact, will be able to speak best if they use their native dialect rather than one that is strange to them. So why should we teach children to speak standard English?

One reason might be that it has been demonstrated that some teachers react more favourably to children who speak standard English than to those who do not. They evaluate the standard English speakers as being more intelligent and having greater academic potential than other children. Since it is also probable that teachers' expectations are a potent factor in affecting a child's performance, we might argue that, if all children spoke standard English, teachers would not be led to discriminate, albeit unconsciously, between children in this way.

It is clear, however, that this would be a very bad reason for teaching children to speak standard English. The correct solution to this problem is surely to point out to teachers and student teachers that they may react in this way, and to encourage them to guard against this kind of reaction. So long as all concerned are persuaded that there is no connection between a child's dialect and his ability, and so long as they are on the look-out for (possibly very subconscious) reactions of a contrary sort, the problem can be avoided.

There is, however, another argument that is worthy of consideration. Even if it is agreed that there are no educational or linguistic disadvantages to speaking non-standard dialects, it is still true that those who speak them may be at a *social* disadvantage in some circumstances. Certain occupations, for example, may be denied to people who do not speak standard English. In other words, it could be said that by not teaching children to speak standard English we are 'keeping them down' and denying them opportunities for 'bettering themselves'. There is undoubtedly some truth in this argument—which is the one most frequently used against the 'appreciation of dialect differences' view. Language can certainly act as a barrier to upward social mobility, although we cannot be sure to what extent. (The barriers are probably much more permeable now than they were.) But even if all teachers were agreed that there was nothing wrong with non-standard dialects, children would still have to be sent out into a world where many employers (and others) react in a very hostile manner to what they still consider to be 'bad English'. Perhaps, therefore, we should attempt to protect working-class and lower middle-class children against the effects of this possible hostility.

(This point of view is probably one major factor behind a notion now gaining ground in some Colleges of Education: that, although notions of 'correctness' in language are without foundation, the idea of 'acceptability' is important. Thus we should no longer say to children that it is *wrong* to say *I done it*, but that it is *not acceptable* (in some circumstances). This may be a step in the right direction, but it is not much of an advance. The notion that some dialects are 'unacceptable' in some circumstances is totally at variance with the concept of dialect tolerance we were advocating earlier. The problem boils down to *who is to say* what is 'acceptable'—and 'acceptable' to who?)

The argument that children should be taught to speak standard English in order to give them a better chance in later life is a laudable one. It is still, however, not a course of action to be recommended, however legitimate the motives behind it. This is because anything a teacher does in the classroom in the way of teaching spoken standard English is likely to be, in nearly all cases, irrelevant. There are two main reasons for this. First, to learn to speak a new dialect of the same language is a difficult task to carry out successfully. Many people are familiar with how difficult it is to learn a foreign language. Even after years of work and practice, it is a rare individual indeed who can speak such a language as well as a native, without betraying his origins as a foreigner. In some ways, of course, learning a new dialect is rather easier than this. The vocabulary, for example, will be more or less the same. But in other crucial respects it is more difficult. The point is that with a new language you start from scratch. But with a new dialect you have to retain some aspects of your native variety while rejecting others—and the big problem is to learn which is which. The two linguistic varieties are so similar that it is difficult to keep them apart. The motivation to learn, moreover, is much smaller. If an English-speaking person learns French, then at least he can communicate with French people and read French books and newspapers. But no communication advantages of this sort arise from learning a new dialect.

Secondly, because of the relationship that exists between dialect and social class, standard English is a variety which is symbolic of membership of a particular social group in our society. This means that to speak standard English is, at least to a certain extent, to align yourself with this social group. The result of this is that no child will trouble to learn to speak standard English as it is taught in school *unless* (*a*) he wants to become associated with the social group that typically speaks standard English, *and* (*b*) he has a reasonable expectation that he will be able to do so. If a child does not want to become a member of the middle or upper echelons of the middle-class (not of course that he will think of it in these terms) or if he does not feel that it is a practicable proposition for someone in his economic and social position to do so, then there is no reason for him to learn to speak standard English, and no way in which he will learn. On the other hand, if a child is so motivated to learn to speak standard English, he will almost certainly do so regardless of whether it is taught in school or not. If he identifies with and comes to associate with standard English speakers, he will learn to speak the dialect from them (and from all the other standard English-using sources) in a relatively automatic and painless way.

We must remember, though, that even he may develop certain problems of a psychological nature as a result of this dialect change. The Norwegian research that we have already mentioned (p. 58) is still in its early stages, but it does suggest that difficulties of this type might occur. It points out that the act of speaking is the result of processes which, except in the case of very young children, take place without conscious attention and are deeply automatic. As soon as attention is directed at processes of this kind, they can no longer be so automatic or spontaneous. Adults may therefore find themselves once again in the position of young children whose rather halting behaviour shows that they have not yet succeeded in rendering these processes fully automatic. In the case of language, if a speaker begins to direct some of his attention to *how* he is speaking, in order to avoid using certain dialect features, his speech will become more hesitant and faltering—and he will also of course be able to pay less attention to *what* he is saying. There is also a possibility that, over a period of time, a speaker will lose fluency in his original dialect, without becoming very competent in the new one. And for some personality types, there is apparently the danger that, in addition to becoming inarticulate, they may develop problems of personal and cultural identity. There may, in other words, be a price to pay for changing one's dialect.

To conclude: the only legitimate motive for teaching children to speak standard English as a second dialect is to prevent them from being discriminated against for speaking socially stigmatised dialects; and the only legitimate method of teaching it is to use the bi-dialectalism approach. But even with this motive, and with this method, the teaching of spoken standard English in school is not advisable, since it is almost certainly a waste of time. Except in cases where children would have learned to speak it anyway, it is very unlikely to succeed; there is a danger of inducing feelings of linguistic insecurity and alienation; and the time spent could certainly be put to better use. We would be much better advised, for example, to concentrate on producing dialect tolerance and linguistic security.

11. Writing

The final argument that we have to deal with is that standard English should be taught in schools so that children can learn to write it. This is an argument which, for the first time, we can

79

accept—up to a point. Once again the only acceptable motive for teaching standard English is that this will do something to prevent children from being discriminated against when they leave school. In the case of the written language, however, it is also a motive we can act upon. The difference is that the teaching of written standard English to children who normally speak some other dialect is likely to achieve some success.

Writing is a very different kind of activity from speaking. It is a much less automatic process. In writing, you can take time to think out what you are going to put down before you commit it to paper, and there is also the possibility of going back afterwards and altering what you have written. For this reason the complexities involved in handling a new dialect are very considerably reduced. There is also much less psychological involvement with the written language than with the spoken: standard English can be regarded as a dialect apart which is used only for writing and which does not commit the writer to allegiance to any particular social group. It will often therefore be possible to encourage children to use standard English grammatical forms in writing that they would be unable or unwilling to use when speaking.

We accept, then, that the teaching of written standard English can be carried out in schools, not because this dialect is 'correct' or even 'appropriate', but because it may be socially and economically advantageous to children when they leave—and because it is possible. We therefore require a careful consideration of when it is useful to write standard English, and when it is not. There is no reason, for example, to ask that children should use standard English in creative writing or in personal letters, since no social advantages are likely to result from this. Children should therefore be free to use whatever grammatical forms come most naturally to them in writing of this sort—particularly since this will free them to concentrate on what they are actually trying to say.

Academic essays, on the other hand, are more problematical. There *is* an advantage to be gained from using standard English in this sort of work, but this is only because when children come to write essays in external examinations, some examiners are likely to mark them down for using non-standard grammar. A top priority, therefore, is to persuade examiners, who are for the most part also teachers and lecturers, that a high-level discussion of, say, the poetry of Keats written in a non-standard dialect is just as good as one in standard English. In particular, examiners can be encouraged to accept that no greater clarity or precision

80

is gained by using a grammatical form from one dialect rather than from another.

But there is a clear case for using standard English in formal and business correspondence, on application forms, and in drafting reports and other 'official' written work. The advantage to be gained is a purely social one, of course, but we have to recognise that, at the moment, most employers and managers will not look kindly on anything written in non-standard dialect. It is therefore helpful to point out to pupils that there are certain types of official writing in which it may be useful to them to employ standard English forms.

THE BI-DIALECTALISM APPROACH

We can agree, then, that the bi-dialectalism approach can be used to teach children who do not normally use standard English how to write it for certain purposes. In order to do this, one thing that is required is that, in looking at children's written work, teachers should distinguish between several different types of 'error'.

First, there will be inadequacies of organisation, lay-out and logical argument. All children are likely to benefit from help with matters of this sort, which have nothing to do with dialect, and are simply a question of presenting one's material in as coherent a way as possible.

Secondly, there will be linguistic defects not connected with dialect differences. A child may show insufficient understanding of what a certain word or phrase means, or of how it is used. Or he may use turns of phrase which are clumsy or do not really form part of the language. All children, again, are likely to write better if they are given help with this kind of problem. (Also under this heading we might consider errors in punctuation and spelling. Punctuation is a useful aid to written expression that all children can probably benefit from acquiring some proficiency in, provided that they have already mastered the actual skill of writing. Some standardisation of spelling is probably also desirable, but it is possible to argue that today we have gone too far in this direction. Many people now regard even a single 'spelling mistake' as incontrovertible evidence of abysmal ignorance, and a great deal of time is spent in some schools on teaching uniform spelling. English spelling is, in some cases, so arbitrary that a greater degree of flexibility would be welcome. At earlier periods in our history, greater variation in spelling was tolerated, and this appears to have caused no problems. Similarly, modern writers of some languages (Norwegian, for instance) habitually employ their own spelling in order to bring it into line with their regional accent—and again no difficulties arise. Probably the main reason why many people concentrate so much on spelling correctly is in order that others will consider them 'educated'. Perhaps we need to broaden somewhat our notions about what it means to be 'educated'!)

Thirdly, some teachers may be concerned about children's use in writing of obviously local turns of phrase and expressions. Here, it may be a good idea to point out that the phrase in question *is* regionally restricted, but, unless comprehension problems are likely to occur, there seems to be no reason why they should not continue to be employed.

Fourthly, we shall probably quite often encounter what might be considered to be 'errors' of *style* (in the sense of the term discussed on p. 19). It is useful for children to understand—as most of them already do to a considerable extent—that informal and colloquial vocabulary can have an impact on the reader quite different from that produced by formal vocabulary. And it may be also helpful for teachers to point out that while, for example, *bloke, man* and *gentleman* all mean much the same thing, they have very different connotations, and that there are different social conventions about their use. It is also important to acknowledge, however, that informal vocabulary and 'slang' are never *wrong*. And the use of such vocabulary in, for example, children's readers may have the very useful effect of encouraging children to read simply because they are more familiar with, and can therefore identify better with, the language used—see p. 75.

Finally, there will be errors in standard English due to interference from the child's native dialect. These, of course, will only be considered to be errors in the sort of writing where it has been explicitly stated that standard English should be used—or if the child believes that he is writing standard English. The point is that they are not errors in English, merely in *standard* English. Errors of this sort, naturally enough, will not normally occur in the work of children who already speak standard English as their native dialect.

It is in handling 'errors' of this last type that the bi-dialectalism approach should be used. It is essential, when using this approach, not to give the impression that one sort of English is any better than any other, and to avoid any idea of *correction*. What is involved is, rather, a matter of *converting* one dialect form into another. In the south of England this may involve no more than saying occasionally that forms like *she come* and *them boys* are used in speaking and in, for instance, writing stories, but that in formal letters and the like it is a better idea to write *she came* and *those boys*. In other parts of the country, where differences may be larger, more frequent and perhaps more programmed instruction may be useful. In all areas, however, dialect conversion of this sort is best left until after the child has enough writing ability to be able to turn his attention to what is after all a linguistically rather trivial matter.

Standard English, then, can be taught for certain types of written work, provided that both the methods and the motives are right. At the same time, we must also hope for a future in which dialect tolerance will be extended even to the written language. One way of working towards this is for teachers to show that there are (or ought to be) no taboos about the use of non-standard grammar in written work. For instance, when children are dictating sentences for the teacher to write down— in working on the blackboard or in helping slow writers—it is helpful if the teacher puts down *exactly* what the child says, regardless of dialect. It is very encouraging to see sentences like *We never done that before* appearing boldly in the teacher's handwriting in a child's exercise book. In addition to promoting the 'appreciation of dialect differences' approach this also helps to give a child confidence in expressing himself in writing in his own way— before he goes on to refinements like using standard English. The reading and writing scheme *Breakthrough to Literacy*, developed by the Schools Council Programme in Linguistics and English Teaching, sets out to do exactly this. It is designed to help the child develop reading and writing skills at the same time, and encourages him to produce and write his own materials, based on his own spoken language, in his own native dialect. In this way, children do not find themselves in a situation where they are suddenly confronted with unfamiliar language, and they are able to use their native dialects in written work without acquiring an inferiority complex about it.

12. English as a world language

The arguments above have all centred on the child or on the school. There is one further argument we should consider that is rather broader in scope. This is that English is a *world language* of considerable importance in communication, and that we should therefore insist on standard English in schools so that (*a*) there is no danger of a breakdown in communication in the English-speaking world, and (*b*) foreigners learning and using English should have some standard to go by. As far as the first point is concerned, we have already stated, in Chapter 1, that there is no danger of English fragmenting to the point of loss of communication. On the contrary, in the modern situation, convergence is much more probable than divergence. We cannot say, then, as some people believe, that it is only a dedicated band of school-teachers that is managing to hold the English language together.

As far as foreigners using English is concerned we can say this: we are not advocating, in this book, the abolition of standard English. Indeed, it is clear that standard English is a dialect that is in no danger of dying out in the foreseeable future. And even if it *were* to disappear, grammatical differences between English dialects are generally so trivial, as we have said before, that foreigners would be very unlikely to suffer comprehension difficulties on this score, once they had decided which dialect of the language they were going to learn.

There is no need, then, to place an extra burden on the shoulders of British children simply because English is a 'world language'.

13. The special position of some West Indian children

We have said above that dialect differences in Britain are not large enough to cause serious reading or comprehension difficulties. There is, however, an exception. Some, but by no means all, children of West Indian origin may have problems of this type. Some West Indian children, in fact, may be faced with what can best be called a semi-foreign language problem.

The language spoken in many parts of the West Indies is referred to by some people as 'English' but by others by some other name such as 'creole' or 'patois'. This uncertainty of terminology is the result of the problem of drawing boundaries between dialects and languages that we discussed in Chapter 1. The fact is that many of the dialects spoken in the West Indies, although clearly related to English, are nevertheless very different from British English, to the extent that they may not be comprehensible to British listeners at all. In this sort of situation, it is not really possible to make an objective decision about whether West Indians speak 'English' or not.

The situation varies from island to island, but in many places some people—particularly the educated middle-class—speak something that clearly is English, while some at the other end of the social scale speak something that clearly is not—but people at intermediate social levels speak something in between, which is really where the problem lies. There is also stylistic variation from context to context.

The position is further complicated by the fact that many West Indians, naturally enough, feel rather insulted if they are told that they do not speak English. They have always regarded themselves as English-speakers, and English is a 'world language' with high status, while, say, Jamaican Creole (if we choose to regard it as a separate language) is not. (There is also the point that, as we have said, many West Indians *do* speak a variety that is unambiguously English.) Unfortunately, moreover, their similarity to (but clear difference from, in many cases) British dialects has led some people to suppose that West Indian dialects are some kind of 'corrupt' or 'debased' form of English. This, of course, is not so. It just happens that West Indians speak a collection of dialects which, for a number of complex historical reasons, bear, to different degrees, a close resemblance to other dialects normally called 'English' to the extent that it is not possible to put a dividing line anywhere and say 'this is English, but this isn't'. It is therefore very important to stress that, whatever name we choose to give them, West Indian dialects are all entirely adequate and perfectly normal forms of language.

Our concern here, however, is with West Indian children in British schools. The language they use actually varies very considerably, depending on where in the West Indies their family comes from; what social background they have; how long they or their family have lived in this country; what proportion of the people they associate with are West Indian; and to what extent they identify with West Indian or British culture. Many West Indian children, too, are very competent 'bi-dialectals'.

With some immigrant children from other areas, such as Pakistan and India, we know, linguistically speaking, where we are. English is a foreign language for them which we do not expect them to understand until they have learnt it—and we supply special classes and centres to help them do so. But with West

Indian children we cannot be sure. Some speak a British English dialect; some speak 'pure patois'; and many speak something in between. Some, then, will have a semi-foreign language problem, to varying extents, and others will not—and one big problem, of course, is to decide which is which.

In the case of a child whose native West Indian dialect is radically different from British English, and who has had little exposure to British dialects, the following problems may occur:

1. Teachers may find that they have difficulty in understanding what a child is saying. It is important that this should be recognised as the result of dialect differences, and not ascribed to some pathological problem or speech defect. The child is not a case for a speech therapist. Nor is there any reason to teach him to speak British English. Given time, he will probably make the necessary adjustments himself. What is required, rather, is concentration and patience on the part of the teacher.

2. The child may have difficulty in understanding the teacher. The danger here is that this will be put down to lack of intelligence on the part of the child—and this is almost certainly one explanation for the high proportion of West Indian children in schools for the educationally sub-normal. It may also help to account for the high proportion of West Indian children in schools for the deaf. The important thing is to recognise that the child is having difficulties of the same sort that an Indian or Pakistani child may have—although normally not so severe. (However, it is probably *semi*-comprehension that sometimes gives the false impression of lack of intelligence. If a child understands *nothing*, it will be clear to everyone that language difficulties may be responsible. But this is not nearly so apparent if the child understands *something*.) Again, what is required here is patience and understanding of the problem. Given time, the child's problems with understanding British English will decrease.

3. The child may have problems in learning to read and write because of the mechanical difficulties caused by the often considerable dialect differences. Here, some knowledge of West Indian dialects on the part of the teacher might be useful for predicting what difficulties are likely to arise. Problems of this type should also be taken into consideration when assessing a child's academic performance.

It is also worth noting that research that has been carried out recently has suggested that some West Indian children whose language appears to be very British, and who are known to be good readers, may still understand less of what they read than other children, because of subtle grammatical and vocabulary differences between West Indian and British varieties. There might, therefore, be a case for special 'British English' classes for those West Indian children, particularly newly arrived teen-agers, who felt they might benefit from them. Once again, we must point out that the problem is not just one with *standard* English, but with all British dialects.

What is more important, though, is to persuade West Indian and British people alike that there is nothing inferior, 'broken' or to be ashamed of in the dialects spoken by West Indians. We also need to inform teachers that some of their West Indian children may be having problems because British English is partly a foreign language to them, and that they may therefore require a certain amount of sympathetic consideration on some occasions. Above all, perhaps, care must also be taken not to heighten any possible cultural conflicts by rejecting, correcting or decrying West Indian dialect forms.

5 Non-standard dialect, restricted code, and verbal deprivation

It is one of the major themes of this book that there is nothing wrong or inadequate about the language of normal children. So far we have discussed this point only with reference to accents and dialects, but there are many people in education who, even if they are persuaded that all dialects and accents are equally good, still believe that the language of some children is inadequate in other, perhaps more fundamental ways.

Any discussion of this supposed inadequacy normally centres around one or both of two topics: the work of Basil Bernstein; and the 'verbal deprivation' hypothesis. Linguists have serious doubts about the former, and are convinced that the latter is not valid. Whatever the merits of the two sets of theories, however, it is important to appreciate that neither has any connection with differences in grammatical forms between linguistic varieties. They have nothing to do, that is, with differences between standard English and other dialects.

This means that the topic of this chapter has, in theory, no connection with the subject matter of the book as a whole: accents and dialects. In fact, however, there are a number of important reasons for discussing this matter here. First, it is a subject of such importance in the field of language and education that we cannot afford to ignore it. Secondly, it is a controversial topic to which the results of linguistic research can usefully be applied. And, thirdly, many people have mistakenly come to believe that there is some connection between this supposedly more fundamental inadequacy, on the one hand, and differences of dialect, on the other. We therefore have to attempt to show that there is not.

In this chapter, then, we shall try to argue that there *is* no such fundamental inadequacy in the language of certain children, and that, even if there were, it would have no connection with differences of dialect—and could not therefore be used as an argument for teaching children to use standard English as well as or instead of their native dialects.

1. Bernstein

Basil Bernstein is Professor in the Sociology of Education at the London University Institute of Education. His work, although it has been widely misunderstood, has been extremely influential in educational circles, and his theories are often taught as accepted orthodoxy in Colleges and Institutes of Education. His work has generally been of greatest interest to educationists, sociologists and psychologists, but recently linguists have also begun to take note of Bernstein's writings. In fact, most linguists, including myself, now find that they disagree with, or at least feel very sceptical about, Bernstein's work, especially his earlier articles which have had the greatest influence.

In the late 1950s and early 1960s Bernstein developed a theory about the relationship between language and social class. He postulated that there were two different varieties of language which he called 'elaborated code' and 'restricted code'. And he attempted to demonstrate that whereas middle-class children use both these 'codes', some, but by no means all, working-class children use only 'restricted code'.

How does one recognise these 'codes'? It is actually rather difficult to say, since Bernstein has rarely given examples of any length, but he has listed a number of the characteristics of the two codes, only some of which are purely linguistic. 'Restricted code', for example, is characterised linguistically by features such as a high proportion of personal pronouns (especially *you* and *they*); by tag-questions such as 'didn't you?' and 'isn't it?'; and by the relative infrequency of subordinate clauses and passive verbs. 'Elaborated code' is characterised by a relatively high proportion of adverbs, conjunctions, subordinate clauses and passive verbs.

According to Bernstein, 'restricted code' is typically used within groups who know each other well, such as families, and it has the effect of stressing the speaker's membership of that group. Speakers using 'restricted code' also take a number of shared assumptions for granted, rather than making them explicit. 'Elaborated code', on the other hand, tends to be used in more formal situations; it stresses the speaker's individuality as a person; and it takes less for granted.

The degree of the impact of Bernstein's research has been rather remarkable. The most important reason for this is that it seemed initially to provide an at least partial explanation for the disturbing under-achievement of working-class children in school. This phenomenon was, and still is, extremely worrying to many teachers, and here now was a theory that appeared to supply, depending on how you looked at it, either a solution to the problem, or an excuse for the relative failure of the school. If the educational situation required children to use 'elaborated code' and some working-class children did not use it, then it was obvious why their school performance was relatively inferior. Bernstein himself made this point explicitly. He argued, for example, that children 'limited' to 'restricted code' would be less able to generalise and more likely to emphasise the concrete at the expense of the abstract. After Bernstein had published his earlier papers, therefore, it seemed to some educationists that a solution to their problems was at hand: working-class children should be taught to use 'elaborated code'. Others, less optimistic, now felt that children without 'elaborated code' were simply less educable and that there was little one could do about it. But from both points of view, Bernstein's theories were very welcome.

Unfortunately, a number of very important criticisms have subsequently been made of Bernstein's original studies which have the effect of nullifying them, at least to a very considerable extent. First, it has to be asked whether there really are such linguistic entities as 'elaborated' and 'restricted codes'. The linguistic characteristics of the codes which Bernstein cites are really only tendencies, and they include many of the features which linguists would normally associate with differences of style (see p. 19). (This is particualrly true of the characteristic concerning the proportion of passive verbs, for instance.) If it is simply a matter of styles under another name, then—since styles are generally considered to be equivalent but less or more formal ways of saying the same thing—it is hard to imagine what educational effect this can have. In any case, Bernstein has now almost abandoned the term 'code', at least in its original sense.

Secondly, it has never been made clear exactly how linguistic features such as passive verbs and subordinate clauses can affect a child's ability to generalise and handle abstractions, to the extent that this has an effect on his educational performance. Most of

90

the work that has been carried out into the relationship between language and thought processes is speculative and controversial. Although there clearly is a connection between thought and language, no one has succeeded in showing precisely what it is. We can therefore have no confidence at all that Bernstein's 'codes', if there are such things, have any effect on cognition. (Equally, of course, we cannot be certain that they do not.)

Thirdly, we have to ask exactly what is meant by any statement which suggests that the educational situation requires the ability to use 'elaborated code'. In the absence of any concrete evidence in favour of the educational benefits of 'elaborated code', it is legitimate to suggest that, if there is such a 'requirement', it is simply that some teachers expect academically successful children to use middle-class ways of talking and writing and therefore have higher expectations of those who do. The 'requirement', that is, may really be little more than a convention.

Fourthly, it has been shown by other researchers that working-class children *can* use 'elaborated code', as defined by Bernstein, particularly in writing. Bernstein's earlier papers, in fact, are based on only a small amount of experimentation into children's ability to produce different 'codes', and he has been particularly criticised for failing to take into account, in the research he did carry out, several situational factors which effect linguistic performance. Subsequent workers were thus able to manipulate situations so that children *did* produce 'elaborated code'. We discuss this further below, but it should be obvious to most people that a formal, artificial, tape-recorded discussion of capital punishment—Bernstein's first and for a time only experiment—is much more likely to produce confident discussion from public-school boys than from post-office messengers—as indeed it did.

Fifthly, the most serious criticism of Bernstein's work is the effect it has had on the ideas many teachers and others have about working-class language. It has fostered or, in some cases, strengthened the belief that there is something intrinsically inferior about working-class language. Bernstein himself does not actually believe this, but he has succeeded in giving very many people the impression that he does. This is due to a considerable extent to his use in the earlier papers of adjectives such as 'restricted', 'limited', 'poor', and 'rigid', and to the suggestion that there is 'something lacking' in working-class language—namely 'elaborated code'. The view has therefore grown up that educational failure is due to an inadequacy in the child himself—in his language —rather than to any other cause such as the school or the system.

Bernstein's work, in fact, is notable for the way in which it has been misunderstood, misinterpreted and misused. (He does write at a very high level of abstraction, with almost no linguistic examples to illustrate or prove his points. And his style of writing puts many obstacles in the way of full comprehension for those unused to it.) There are two major misconceptions surrounding Bernstein's work. One is that 'restricted code' has some connection with non-standard dialect. The other is that there is a phenomenon known as 'verbal deprivation'.

2. 'Restricted code' and non-standard dialect

It is widely believed that 'restricted' and 'elaborated code' have something to do with dialect and even accent. Many people appear to think that non-standard dialects and 'restricted code' are one and the same thing. This is emphatically not so. Bernstein's 'codes' have no connection whatsoever with dialect. Proportions of relative clauses, passive verbs, adverbs and so on have nothing to do with the grammatical differences that we have discussed as differentiating between social-class dialects.

The form, say, a personal pronoun takes in particular dialects (*himself* as opposed to *hisself*, for example) has no connection whatsoever with the proportion of personal pronouns a speaker happens to use. The former is a feature of dialect, the latter a feature of 'code'. According to Bernstein, speakers switch from one code to another without switching dialects; and it is just as possible for non-standard dialect speakers to use 'elaborated code' as it is for standard dialect speakers to use 'restricted code'.

At some points Bernstein's early papers are somewhat unclear on this subject, but most of the responsibility for this misconception rests with other authors. A notable offender here is Andrew Wilkinson. In his book *The Foundations of Language*, he gives invented examples of the two 'codes'. The 'restricted code' example begins:

'So me and Mike goes down to the museum . . .'

while the 'elaborated code' version starts off:

'So Mike and I went down to the museum . . .'.

Neither of these examples contains, up to this point, any of the features supposedly characteristic of the two 'codes'. Rather, the first version contains one non-standard grammatical form (*goes* rather than *go*) and two features typical of informal styles (*me and Mike* rather than *Mike and I*; and the use of the narrative present tense rather than the past: *goes* rather than *went*). The 'elaborated code' passage has the equivalent standard dialect and formal style forms. Wilkinson thereby gives the impression that there is some necessary connection between 'code' and dialect—which there is not. According to Bernstein's list of 'code' features, a sentence such as:

The blokes what was crossing the road got knocked down by a car

has characteristics of 'elaborated code' (a subordinate clause and a passive verb), whereas

The gentlemen were crossing the road and a car knocked them down

does not. The former, we can say, is non-standard dialect, with informal vocabulary, but 'elaborated code'; while the latter is standard dialect, with more formal vocabulary, but *not* 'elaborated code'.

The current confusion of 'restricted code' with non-standard dialect in the minds of many teachers and educationists is particularly unfortunate. It has meant that, at a time when many people in education are beginning to recognise that non-standard dialects are in no way inferior, others have simply had their prejudices about non-standard speech reinforced. It appears, in fact, that some educationists, many no doubt unwittingly, have misused Bernstein's theories in order to lend unfounded notions about 'bad' and 'incorrect' language an air of apparent academic respectability. This has meant that those who believe that working-class dialects are inferior have been able to drop the no-longer respectable assertion that they are 'wrong' and to claim instead that they are 'restricted'.

Their argument runs something like this: Bernstein has shown that middle-class language is 'elaborated' and working-class language is 'restricted'. Working-class language is therefore inferior to middle-class language, and since working-class language consists of non-standard dialects, these dialects must be inferior. Working-class children should therefore be taught to speak and write standard English instead.

This argument is unsound on all counts. Even if we accept

the validity of Bernstein's theory of 'codes'—which, as I have said, many linguists are reluctant to do—we have to note that Bernstein has never actually claimed that 'elaborated code' is superior to 'restricted' code'. It is true, though, that it is difficult not to draw this conclusion from some of his writings—particularly since, for example, children who do not use 'elaborated code' are said to be 'limited'. The main point, however, is that even if we were to accept that 'elaborated code' both exists *and* is superior to 'restricted code', this could still not be used as an argument for suggesting that standard English is superior to other dialects. It is not—and Bernstein's theories cannot legitimately be employed to demonstrate that it is. Dialects and codes are entirely independent entities, and non-standard dialects are *not* 'restricted code'.

3. Verbal deprivation

The second major misconception that has arisen partly out of the work of Bernstein is that some working-class children are 'verbally deprived'. To say that this is a misunderstanding of Bernstein is perhaps to be rather charitable, since he does in his earlier articles use the term *deprivation* in a language context. In his later works, however, he has explicitly stated that working-class children are not 'verbally deprived'.

The 'verbal deprivation' or 'language deficit' hypothesis is due mainly to the work of educational psychologists in the United States. The hypothesis is that the language of certain working-class children is inadequate. They have, according to this view, been 'deprived' of language, as a result of which they also suffer from a 'cognitive deficit'. (This link between language and cognition is of course very controversial anyway—see above p. 91.) Whether or not the term 'restricted code' is actually used, it is said that characteristics of the working-class child's language produce differences in his interpretation of the world and ability to organise his experience *vis-à-vis* middle-class children. It is claimed that working-class language is not adequate for dealing with certain sorts of concepts and modes of thinking, and that working-class children are therefore not able to perform logical operations or handle abstractions. Working-class children are also said to be 'non-verbal': they are unable to express themselves, inarticulate, and say very little.

Supporters of the 'verbal deprivation' hypothesis have also

94

suggested an explanation for this 'linguistic deficit': working-class children grow up in a 'linguistically deprived environment'. It is said that these children receive little verbal stimulation; that their mothers do not talk to them; that their homes are noisy; that communication takes the form, in working-class homes, of shouts, clichés, and gestures; and that the children hear little well-formed language.

Linguists hold a view that is radically opposed to this—particularly since many of them have worked on or followed research which has dealt with and described working-class children and homes which bear little or no resemblance to those described by the verbal deprivationists. As the well-known and highly respected American linguist William Labov has written, in connection with the claim that some children are verbally deprived: 'The evidence put forward for this claim is transparently wrong, as linguists unanimously agree'. There is thus no disagreement among linguists that 'verbal deprivation' is a myth—and a dangerous myth, at that. This, of course, is strong language for an academic discussion, but unfortunately this is an issue on which one cannot afford to mince words, since some of the consequences of the 'verbal deprivation' hypothesis have been very serious indeed. This is particularly true in the U.S.A., where a number of so-called compensatory education programmes have been set up with the aim of, amongst other things, 'giving' language to children who have been 'deprived' of it. These programmes, as well as costing a great deal of money, have in some cases had the effect of stigmatising some children (in America mostly Blacks) as inherently inferior, and of diverting attention from real defects in the educational system.

There are also signs, however, that some British educationists and psychologists are accepting 'verbal deprivation' as established fact. For example, in his book *Language and Teaching* Peter Herriot has a chapter entitled 'Language Deficit and Remediation' in which he specifically links 'restricted code' with 'language deficit'—as I have tried to point out, a misunderstanding of Bernstein. Similarly, Andrew Wilkinson uses quite freely the terms 'linguistically deprived' and 'linguistically disadvantaged', while J. Patrick Creber, in his book unfortunately titled *Lost for Words*, has a chapter called 'Language Deprivation in School'. And another author who explicitly links Bernstein with 'linguistic deprivation' is F. D. Flower in his book *Language and Education* (p. 110).

How did this unfortunate state of affairs come about? One important factor is certainly that the strongest proponents of the verbal deprivation hypothesis are psychologists and others who have carried out little linguistic research and are not very knowledgeable about the nature of language. A good example of this is provided by the argument that working-class children receive little 'verbal stimulation' at home. Most of the 'evidence' for this is either anecdotal or based on inadequate stereotypes. Very little of it is based on direct observation. Linguists who have been involved in urban dialect surveys and other sociolinguistic research have spent considerable amounts of time actually inside working-class homes recording language as it is used there. They therefore have tape-recorded evidence that children in this type of home receive very considerable 'verbal stimulation' and that complex verbal activities of different sorts are continually in progress.

Advocates of the 'verbal deprivation' hypothesis also manifest a sometimes surprising degree of ignorance about language itself. Herriot writes, for example:

> Investigations of younger children show that working-class three and four year-olds use much larger units as grammatical items. Grammatical skill in middle-class children involves the ordering of morphemes; but in working-class children of the same age it involves the ordering of groups of morphemes. The working-class child, in other words, has a limited number of phrase-sized units, and therefore many fewer combinations of items are open to him. For example, he may say 'That big dog' as a single unit, having to miss out the auxiliary 'is' and the article 'a' in order to remember it all. This sentence is a unit for him, and so he has to say 'That big dog, that little dog' if he wishes to compare dogs. For the middle-class child, however, the morphemes are the units he orders grammatically; so he can say 'That's a big dog, but this isn't', or 'Isn't that a big dog?' or 'That's a big dog, isn't it?'

There is no linguistic evidence whatsoever to justify assertions of this sort. As far as linguists working with child language acquisition are aware, no child treats 'that big dog' as a single grammatical unit. (Note that the morpheme can be defined as the smallest grammatical unit. For example, the phrase *The running dogs* consists of the morphemes: *the*; *run*; *-ing*; *dog*; *-s*. Linguists' reactions to this paragraph of Herriot's range from 'misguided' to 'ludicrous'. Elsewhere in the book Herriot makes other elementary linguistic errors.)

96

In a similar vein, Creber produces a list of 'language habits of the disadvantaged'. The list contains a number of unwarranted claims, including the assertion that the disadvantaged child 'speaks in a very limited vocabulary'. This is a comment that is frequently made about working-class children, but again it has received no support from any research data. In fact, all normal children of school age have a vocabulary that is very large indeed —several thousand words at least. Moreover, it is in practice impossible to discover how many words any individual knows, particularly since there will normally be a marked difference between active and passive vocabulary. It is almost certainly true, however, that different children will have differently developed vocabularies on different topics—depending on their interests and experience. Children who are not interested in school may therefore have a relatively small 'school vocabulary', but this should not be equated with lack of total vocabulary. A very interesting exercise would be to compare the vocabulary range and fluency of working-class children talking about, say, their favourite football team with that of their middle-class peers.

Some American proponents of 'verbal deprivation' have also attempted to link 'deprivation' to non-standard dialects. It has been suggested, for example, that American Black English dialects are less 'logical' than standard English. We have already discussed and dismissed this argument in Chapter 4. All dialects of English are merely equivalent in this respect.

Another important factor in the development of the 'verbal deprivation' hypothesis has undoubtedly been the testing situation. As Labov has pointed out, much of the evidence which has led to the concept of 'the non-verbal child' is based on interviews conducted by educational psychologists with one child at a time in what to the child are very alien and artificial surroundings:

> 'The child is in an asymmetrical situation where anything he says can literally be held against him. He has learned a number of devices to *avoid* saying anything in this situation, and he works very hard to achieve this end. One may observe the intonation patterns . . . which Negro children often use when they are asked a question to which the answer is obvious. The answer may be read as "Will this satisfy you?" '

If interviews of this type are taken, Labov says,

> 'as a measure of the verbal capacity of the child, it must be as his capacity to defend himself in a hostile and threatening

situation. But unfortunately, thousands of such interviews are used as evidence of the child's total verbal capacity'.

Linguists who have carried out research into language as it is actually used in everyday life have been very aware of this kind of problem. The difficulty for the linguist is that he wants to observe the way people speak when they are not being observed. If speakers know that someone is studying or recording their speech, they normally alter it in some way—they may try and be more 'correct', for example. Linguists have therefore taken pains to set up situations where speakers feel at ease, forget they are being tape-recorded, and talk freely and normally. This is most likely to happen if the setting is an informal one—not an interview— and if a group of people are all recorded together. The best and most natural recordings of working-class children have been made outside contexts like the school and home (which are adult-dominated) with groups of youngsters playing or talking together.

In this kind of setting, linguists have obtained large amounts of spontaneous and often coherent, logical, graphic and skilful speech. They are therefore agreed that the 'non-verbal child' is, at least, a very rare animal (and they will surely be supported in this by all those teachers who have problems with children who will not stop talking rather than vice versa). The fact is, and this has important implications for the school—that no one uses language to the best of their ability unless they are in a situation in which they feel comfortable and relaxed.

4. Bernstein's later work

This last point is very relevant to Bernstein's studies. Nearly all his work has involved the observation of children in artificial testing situations—situations which are less alien to middle-class than to working-class children. Testers themselves tend to be middle-class. And many middle-class children are encouraged by their parents to become used to situations where they are asked to answer questions, the answers to which are already obviously known to the person doing the asking—an otherwise rather artificial exercise. Many of Bernstein's discussions of working-class language must therefore be seen in this light.

This and other criticisms of his work have been discussed by Bernstein in his later articles. He has recently, for example, devoted considerable attention to the effect of situation. But he now suggests that the experimental situation is in many respects typical of the school, and that it is therefore possible to generalise from a child's performance in the experiment to how he will perform in school. One implication that can be drawn from this is diametrically opposed to the implication which many educationists chose to draw from Bernstein's earlier 'restricted' and 'elaborated code' papers. The new implication is that the school (or at least some schools) do not provide the kind of social context in which working-class children are able (or willing) to use language most effectively. In other words, the problem *can* now be viewed as resting with the school and not with the child or his language.

Other modifications to the earlier theories also appear. The two 'codes', for example, are now seen not as separate varieties but rather as tendencies, and have also become more abstract and less linguistic. Different types of family structure, moreover, are now regarded as a more important differentiating factor than social class. Bernstein suggests that 'positional' families, where your status as 'father', 'youngest daughter' etc. is the most important factor in deciding your role in the family, are less likely to give rise to 'the verbal elaboration of individual differences' than 'personal' families, where an individual's personality and abilities are more important than his status—where, in other words, *who* you are is more important that *what* you are. More attention is now also paid to evidence demonstrating that working-class children may be less *explicit* than middle-class children in their use of language. Once again, however, much of the evidence for this has been obtained in testing situations where the information explicitly given by the middle-class children was for the most part redundant. For example, when presented with a picture to describe, working-class children tended to say 'he' whereas middle-class children were more likely to say 'the man'. The point is that, since both the children and the person they were describing the picture to could *see* the picture (i.e. the exercise was a very artificial one), it was obvious to all concerned who 'he' was.

5. Summary

We can say that, from the point of view of most linguists, Bernstein's earlier theories of 'elaborated' and 'restricted codes' are very suspect. His later theories have not so far been rejected out of hand, but many linguists are at present sceptical about them.

What may well be true is that speakers from different social class backgrounds have different access to different styles. One reason for this might be that working-class people are generally less used to participating in formal situations. This, however, is more a problem of social conventions than of educability. It is also doubtless true that there are various language activities—such as persuading, describing, narrating, and so on—which children can be helped to develop in school and which some children may be more experienced at than others. But this is a matter of language *use*, and lack of ability at persuading, for example, does not mean that there is anything wrong with the child's language as such.

All linguists are agreed that there is no foundation for the notion of 'verbal deprivation'. We can say that, just as it is not legitimate to suggest that we ought to change children's dialects because those they already have are 'wrong', so it is not valid to claim that we ought to try to 'give' children language because they have been 'deprived' of it. We stated above, of course, that there is essentially no connection, although some American educationists have tried to make one, between the notion of 'verbal deprivation', on the one hand, and the question of dialect differences, on the other. In practice, however, there is a link: the 'elimination' approach to non-standard dialects may produce speakers who, in some situations, appear to be 'non-verbal', simply because their confidence in the value of their native dialects has been undermined, and they are reluctant to say anything lest they 'make a mistake'.

In the educational situation we therefore require three things. First, a recognition of the fact that speakers may not operate very well linguistically in situations which are strange to them. This may be because they have not had sufficient practice in using the linguistic varieties normally used in these situations. (It is probably an open question as to what extent these varieties— styles—are in some way useful or are simply a matter of social convention.) But it is also certainly because they do not feel socially comfortable or at ease.

Secondly, we require the cultivation of a 'language climate' in schools which will allow pupils to feel at ease in expressing their own ideas and discussing problems as freely as they can. What is needed, in other words, is a social situation where, as far as possible, teachers and pupils feel that the use of language and the mutual exchange of ideas can take place without the fear that one is talking out of turn, breaking rules, or losing control. The general atmosphere, that is, should be one that will encourage talk.

Thirdly—and this has been the main thesis of this book—we require the development of dialect and accent tolerance on the part of teacher and pupil alike. Language will be employed best and most effectively if both speaker and hearer feel free to ignore the dialect characteristics of what is being said and concentrate instead on its content.

6. Postscript

In this chapter we have been able to deal only very briefly with an important and controversial subject that is worthy of a whole book in itself. Wider reading on this topic is therefore particularly recommended. Further discussion can be found in the important papers by William Labov (on 'verbal deprivation') and Harold Rosen (on Bernstein) listed in the *Further Reading* section. And for the views of a linguist more sympathetic to Bernstein, see Michael Halliday's Introduction to *Class, Codes and Control*, Vol. 2.

6 Conclusion

I have tried to show in this book that there is only one legitimate reason for teaching standard English in schools: in order that children should not be discriminated against for using low-status dialects. I have also suggested that the teaching of standard English should be confined to certain sorts of written work; and that the bi-dialectalism approach should be used to teach it. More importantly, I have also tried to argue that, at the same time, we should do all we can to advance the progress of the 'appreciation of dialect differences' view. And I have put forward reasons for allowing and indeed encouraging children to speak and write in their own native dialects.

Paradoxically perhaps, although this book has been concerned with linguistic diversity, it is my hope that it will help to direct attention away from differences of accent and dialect towards more important issues. We should, I suggest, no longer concern ourselves with topics such as 'bad grammar' and 'slovenly speech'. Rather, we should concentrate on other matters. More attention, for example, can be paid to literacy. (It may help here to persuade children that their own dialects are good and interesting so that they are less inclined to dissociate themselves from any activity that has to do with language.) And we can also perhaps devote more time to what are sometimes called 'verbal skills'. Care does have to be taken here. We must be clear that all normal school-age children already *have* language, and that there is nothing inadequate or defective about it. We must also recognise that they already have very many useful and impressive verbal skills. But we can still give them additional opportunities for taking part in and developing verbal activities such as persuading, arguing, discussing, protesting, describing, narrating—and all the other activities it is useful to be able to employ language for.

Above all, though, by not criticising their 'bad grammar' or 'slovenly speech', we can encourage children from all areas and classes to become confident speakers and writers who can express themselves clearly and without embarrassment, and who are articulate users of English which is, in the true sense of the word, good.

Further Reading

Works marked with an asterisk are recommended for further reading by those interested in the particular topics. The other works are included for reference—for the very interested or the very sceptical.

CHAPTER 1

Those readers who are interested in linguistic change in English are referred to B. Strang *A History of English* (Methuen) which is now available in paperback, while those who feel they might like to know more about linguistics can consult D. Crystal *What is linguistics?* (Arnold).

CHAPTER 2

Some of the sociolinguistic research mentioned in this chapter is discussed at greater length in P. Trudgill *Sociolinguistics: An Introduction* (Penguin). The Detroit data is taken from R. Shuy et al. *Linguistic Correlates of Social Stratification in Detroit Speech* (U.S. Office of Education), while the Norwich figures can be found in P. Trudgill *The Social Differentiation of English in Norwich* (C.U.P.). Information on the Bradford area was provided by K. M. Petyt of the Reading University Department of Linguistic Science, from his research data, and the Glasgow figures appear in R. Macaulay & G. Trevelyan *Language, Education and Employment in Glasgow* (Social Science Research Council Report). New York scores are from W. Labov *The Social Stratification of English in New York City* (Center for Applied Linguistics), while the Reading data comes from surveys carried out by students at Reading University.

A discussion of the apparently aesthetic merits of different accents can be found in H. Giles et al. 'The imposed norm hypothesis: a validation' (*Quarterly Journal of Speech*, October 1974). An excellent work on grammar, in the true sense of this term, is